27 July 2011

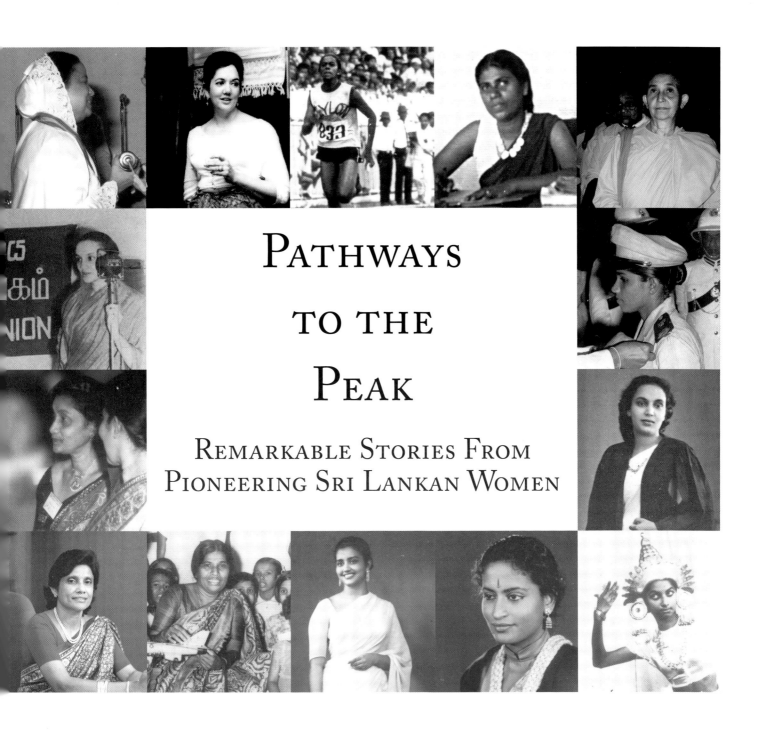

Pathways to the Peak

Remarkable Stories From Pioneering Sri Lankan Women

Published by the Bay Owl Press, 2011
an imprint of the Perera Hussein Publishing House
www.ph-books.com

First edition

ISBN: 978-955-1723-23-1

All rights reserved

© Dinusha Panditaratne and Shalini Panditaratne

The right of Dinusha Panditaratne and Shalini Panditaratne to be identified as the authors of this work has been asserted by them in accordance with the Copyright, Designs & Patents Act.

This book is sold subject to the condition that it shall not, by way of trade or otherwise, be lent, re-sold, hired out, copied, extensively quoted or otherwise circulated, in any form of binding or cover other than that in which it is published, without the express written permission of the publisher.

All photographs and pictures were provided to the authors for publication by the individuals profiled in this book from their personal collections.

Layout by Lindsay Morency
Printed by Samayawardhana Printers (Pvt) Ltd.

To offset the environmental pollution caused by printing books,
the Perera Hussein Publishing House grows trees in Puttalam –
Sri Lanka's semi-arid zone.

PATHWAYS TO THE PEAK

Remarkable Stories From Pioneering Sri Lankan Women

Dinusha Panditaratne
&
Shalini Panditaratne

With a foreword by Radhika Coomaraswamy

Message from Finlays

As part of our commitment to sustainable development and in discharging our responsibility to society, we have chosen Education and Women's Empowerment, two out of the eight millennium development goals announced by the United Nations, as our key focal areas. Not forgetting that working women form the large proportion amongst users of our unique, gender based and discreet "Sanitact" service, we feel it is only right to dedicate a part of our Corporate Social Responsibility initiatives, towards improving their working and living conditions.

We are pleased to be associated with this publication on outstanding women of Sri Lanka. Every Sri Lankan woman plays an integral part in uplifting the socio-economic fabric of our country and this is our tribute to them, that they may be inspired by the women who have led the way, for others to follow.

Kumar Jayasuriya
Chairman and Managing Director
Finlays Colombo PLC
Colombo

28th February, 2011

Message from Standard Chartered Bank, Sri Lanka

Diversity and Inclusion lie at the very heart of Standard Chartered Bank's values; and in keeping with these values, we leverage on opportunities to celebrate the success and contribution of women and take pride in supporting this tribute to pioneering women of Sri Lanka.

This collation of role models drawn from all spheres of social contribution will be a source of inspiration to future generations of women, who will surely face challenges in the realization of their dreams. It is a celebration of the journeys and a testimony to the effort and strength of these women.

We congratulate the authors, Shalini and Dinusha, on this beacon to aspiring young women.

Anirvan Ghosh Dastidar
CEO
Standard Chartered Bank, Sri Lanka
20th April, 2011

Contents

Foreword	vii
Preface	x
Anne Abayasekara	16
Barbara Sansoni	28
Bhikkuni Kusuma	40
Jezima Ismail	52
K.G. Badra Gunawardena	64
Kumari Jayawardena	76
Mallika Hemachandra	86
Maureen Seneviratne	96
Premala Sivaprakasapillai Sivasegaram	108
Premila Diwakara	118
Rohini Nanayakkara	126
Stella de Silva	136
Sumitra Peries	148
Vajira Dias	158
Notes	168

Foreword

There is a narrative about Asian women that is dominant in world discourse today that sees us as abused, discriminated against and disempowered. Across the world, in news stories, we are so often depicted as victims, suffering, without any agency. Holding babies to our breast, entreating authoritarian male figures, or sitting silently and looking sad, we seem to be constantly waiting for the world to rescue us.

The world is indeed brutal for some Asian women. Sri Lanka, however, for the most part has escaped some of the worst excesses. Drawing from its Buddhist heritage of equality as well as liberal modern principles, Sri Lanka has done better than most of its neighbours. And yet before 1980, women were still in what seems now to be the modern dark ages. They were grossly underrepresented, if represented at all, in all fields whether it was academia or sports, the arts or the professions. A system of personal laws for the most part discriminated against them in their family life with regard to marriage, divorce and marital property. Labour laws did not protect the most vulnerable of working women. Rape laws were stacked against them so that convictions for sexual violence were rare. Social mores cast aspersions on unmarried women, divorcées and those who were independent of spirit. It was a repressive time where women's identity belonged to men as mothers, wives or daughters.

Despite these constraints and the overwhelming pressure of social convention, there were some extraordinary women who challenged the norms, defied social practice and broke stereotypes. They were overwhelmingly successful and role models for the generations that were to follow. They showed younger women, that they too could reach for their dreams and have a fulfilling public life. They also encouraged women to have an independent economic life which research has shown is the clue to women's safety and security. As the generations that came after them, we must express our gratitude toward their lasting contribution. This book is one such effort, highlighting the lives of a few of these women who have challenged tradition and opened frontiers.

Some of the first institutions to open their doors to women were the universities. There was a time when women academics were very rare and only men were university lecturers. Kumari Jayawardena and her generation changed all that. Until the 1940s, the great historians of Sri Lanka were all male, both native born and foreign. Kumari Jayawardena, though taught by the best of historians both in Sri Lanka and the West went on to break that monopoly and become

Sri Lanka's leading woman historian and social scientist. Her book *Feminism and Nationalism* remains a definitive work, an essential part of the curriculum not only in Sri Lanka but in much of the English speaking world. She would become a mentor for countless young scholars and is probably one of the most acknowledged people in important academic works on Sri Lanka.

Pioneering women also broke into the professions. These were the best and the brightest among women of their era, who went on to university, who pursued degrees and dedicated their lives to public service. They were path breakers and had to strive hard to do things that we now take for granted. Premala Sivaprakasapillai Sivasegaram was the first woman to enter the engineering faculty and to pass out as an engineer. Even today the engineering faculty remains a male bastion and women are a small minority. Stella de Silva, one of Sri Lanka's leading physicians, was one of the few women to pass out as a doctor in her era; today women are equal numbers in the faculty of medicine. Maureen Seneviratne, a fearless attorney at law, was a singular female lawyer of her time; today women dominate the law faculty. Anne Abayasekara was also one of the first journalists who carved a special niche for herself and her writing style. Today women journalists abound.

Though women are present in all the professions today, except perhaps engineering, they occupy the middle tier of employment. They seldom rise to the highest levels of the professions which are still reserved primarily for men. All these women in the present volume however were different. They were not only pioneers but also centres of excellence, the best in their field. Their combination of skill and adventure made them truly special. Women being left behind are especially true in the private sector and in finance and banking. Rohini Nanayakkara and Mallika Hemachandra are the rare women who have penetrated the private sector at the highest levels and made such successes of their lives.

Women artists and sportswomen have also made a great contribution to Sri Lanka and have received international fame and acclaim. Vajira Dias revived Kandyan dance and took the Chitrasena Ballet all over the world to rave reviews. Her Kandyan swan became as sought after as the swan in Swan Lake. Sumitra Peries is a pioneering female director of film with an extraordinary sensibility, making films that truly capture the life experiences of women. She too is a first and a pioneer. Barbara Sansoni harnessed traditional materials and methods in uniquely creative ways. Her artistry continues to win admiration and inspire the imagination of many. Badra Gunawardena made sure women were not kept out of the world of sport. She was the trailblazer for women like Susanthika Jayasinghe who have become today's global athletes.

In the more conservative areas of religion and national security, women have also made inroads. Bhikkuni Kusuma has brought Buddhism into the lives of many women and her gentle and enlightened ways have shown a path to many who needed solace. In the world of the security forces, where women still need to make a prominent breakthrough, Premila Diwakara broke barriers in the police and signalled the fact that many of the violent crimes in the country involved women and children as victims.

Finally women came lately to the world of social activism but now they dominate the field. Jezima Ismail stands out as someone who through the years has fought for vulnerable people and for effective social policy. Kumari Jayawardena and Anne Abayasekara also used their acquired skills to affect the world of social policy. Today women leaders of civil society have taken that mantle and remain the conscience and soul of Sri Lanka, protecting victims, fighting discrimination and working for social peace and harmony.

As a woman who grew up in the generations after these extraordinary women, I realize I owe a great debt to their pioneering spirit and for their trailblazing work. They have all affected our lives and contributed significantly to the development of Sri Lanka. Because of them Sri Lankan women are more liberated, more enlightened and more at peace with themselves. We must thank the authors for bringing forth this volume and for reminding us of our legacy.

Radhika Coomaraswamy

Under-Secretary-General
of the United Nations
Special Representative for
Children and Armed Conflict

9 February 2011

Preface

Storied Lives to Admire, Treasure, and Inspire

There are remarkable stories of women in Sri Lanka that have never been told. Countless women of this country have passed through its ancient and modern times, without any testimony of their ambitions, determination, disappointments, and triumphs. Their lasting contributions went unacknowledged and the path they paved for others remained unlit. With history books chronicling the stories and successes of men, and society divided along expected gendered roles, new generations of girls and women were guided mainly by their immediate social circles, including their parents, siblings, grandmothers, and husbands.

This book is a modest attempt to redress the relative paucity of literature which honours and celebrates extraordinary Sri Lankan women, and which can inspire their younger compatriots. It is based on personal interviews with fourteen such women, whom we as authors were privileged to meet at length, to record personal recollections of their exceptional lives and careers. The interviews and the writing of this volume spanned a number of years, mostly because both authors were living outside Sri Lanka during this period (in Hong Kong and Australia, respectively). Interviews were arranged with selected women on our visits back to the island during the years 2005 to 2010.

This book also represents a personal journey for the authors, who left Sri Lanka together over 35 years ago as a young mother and her infant daughter, to join an awaiting husband and father employed in a faraway land. For that mother, now a grandmother and retired from her own professional career, this book is a way of giving back to the country which provided the education and foundation of her own accomplishments. Equally, for that daughter, who was raised to adulthood almost entirely outside Sri Lanka, this book is a humble tribute to a country which was not formally her own, but which shaped her in a myriad unseen ways. Our decision to write this book reflects our recognition that Sri Lanka's pioneering female achievers positively impacted legions of younger women, both within the country as well as among its extensive diaspora.

There is no doubt that this volume represents only a small sampling of pioneering Sri Lankan women. Besides the great women of antiquity and women leaders of the colonial era, numerous pioneer women of the modern age had already passed away by the time we began this project, leaving us unable to record their own stories. Some have been written about in other books; most significantly, Sirimavo Bandaranaike, who brought enormous and enduring honour to the country by becoming the world's first female head of government. We wish to acknowledge, however, the achievements and contributions of *all* pioneering Sri Lankan women whose lives have already passed. While it would be impossible to name each and every one, just a few examples of such women from more recent times are the architect Minette de Silva, the entomologist Manthri Ramasamy, the performing artist Rukmani Devi, the poet Monica Ruwanpathirana, and the politician Sarojini Yogeswaran.

Equally, we could not include in this volume all living women who are pioneers in their fields, whose inspirational stories deserve to be told. Our aim was to profile a cross-section of older pioneering women in different areas, whose stories risk being lost over time – rather than to present a closed circle of such remarkable women. Many fields of endeavour benefited from having more than one pioneer woman in its midst, even though we could only record the story of a single example. There are also many younger women who are breaking new ground in different occupations (for instance, it was only recently that a woman pilot in Sri Lanka was appointed a captain). As these women are still marching toward the pinnacle of their careers, and will certainly accomplish more, they were not apt for inclusion in this volume.

Consistent with the aim to inspire younger women in Sri Lanka, we interviewed and profiled women who continued to live and work in the country, although there are numerous Sri Lankan women who have admirably achieved pre-eminence abroad. Indeed, one wonders how many *more* pioneering women there would have been in Sri Lanka if not for the drain in human resources which was exacerbated by the civil war from 1983 to 2009. Leadership and excellence tends to congregate around a nation's capital, and this volume features a preponderance of women living in and around Colombo. Yet they hail from different towns and parts of the country, including from Avissawella, Galle, Horana, Jaffna, Kotagala, and Kandy.

The pathbreaking women profiled in this volume attained pre-eminence and shattered preconceptions in richly diverse fields, including in the athletic, artistic, cultural, commercial, educational, professional, scientific, and spiritual spheres. K.G. Badra excelled in a world that few have the physical and mental aptitude to enter – that of internationally competitive sports. A national record holder in running, she represented Sri Lanka in several events at international meets, including at the Commonwealth Games, and brought home several gold medals. In the arts, Sumitra Peries and Vajira Dias are defining names in their respective disciplines of film and dance. The sublime cinematic direction of Sumitra Peries, and the captivating dance and choreography of Vajira Dias, took creative expression in Sri Lanka to new levels of excellence. Films like *Gehenu Lamai* by Sumitra Peries and roles such as 'Sisi' by Vajira Dias in the ballet *Karadiya* are now cultural treasures of Sri Lanka.

Anne Abayasekara was a creative pioneer of another kind, becoming a well-known writer and editor at several influential periodicals, including the *Ceylon Daily News*, *Sunday Observer*, *Sunday Times*, and *Lanka Woman*. Her decades of work as a journalist involved interviewing and informing readers of trailblazing women of the day, a tradition which this book follows. Also in creative endeavours, Barbara Sansoni is a uniquely gifted artist and a noted illustrator. She led the way in designing textiles and other products, and in the process, invigorated the traditional handloom industry to a previously unimaginable extent. The store Barefoot in Colombo stands as a colourful testament to her imaginative compass.

The world of commerce is double-edged for women; relatively easy to enter on a small scale but still difficult to reach its highest strata. Mallika Hemachandra showed that it was possible for a woman to build a dominant business in a major national industry. She single-handedly founded and steered Mallika Hemachandra Jewellers to be a leading force in Sri Lanka's gem and jewellery industry. Rohini Nanayakkara ascended to the highest echelons in the world of banking and finance, becoming the first woman General Manager and Chief Executive Officer of its most venerable national institution, the Bank of Ceylon. In addition, she has served as a director of key public and private organisations, including as a member of the board of several leading companies.

As Nelson Mandela once observed, education is the most powerful weapon which one can use to change the world. This principle is embodied in the lives and careers of Jezima Ismail and Kumari Jayawardena, who are premier educators as well as leaders of social change. Jezima Ismail devoted several decades to educating the country's youth, including as a teacher at Devi Balika Vidyalaya, as Principal of Muslim Ladies' College, and later as Chancellor of the South Eastern University of Sri Lanka. She has led numerous public and non-governmental bodies dedicated to women's issues, development, and human rights in Sri Lanka. Kumari Jayawardena is a national and global intellectual force in the social sciences, particularly in the areas of feminism, ethnicity, and workers' rights. Bridging academia and activism, she has taught and researched at leading tertiary institutions, while also helping to found and lead influential progressive organisations, notably the Social Scientists Association.

There was a time when academically able boys were often urged to be a 'doctor, lawyer, or engineer'. The careers of Stella de Silva, Maureen Seneviratne, and Premala Sivaprakasapillai Sivasegaram made clear that girls too could confidently enter and excel in these professions. Stella de Silva was one of the few women of her time to practise as a doctor. She became a renowned paediatrician, whose expertise healed innumerable children in both public hospitals and private practice. Maureen Seneviratne was a pioneer female lawyer whose outstanding advocacy skills were sought after by clients and colleagues alike. Her illustrious legal career was capped by becoming the first woman to be appointed a President's Counsel. When Premala Sivaprakasapillai Sivasegaram entered the Faculty of Engineering at the University of Ceylon, female engineers were even rarer than today. Yet she graduated with first class honours, and rose to the position of Chief Structural Engineer at the Buildings Department.

Premala Sivaprakasapillai Sivasegaram succeeded in a scientific sphere which is still widely regarded as a male domain. Similarly, Premila Diwakara and Kusuma Devendra broke through the ranks in fields that are still commonly viewed as 'unsuitable' for women. Premila Diwakara was among a handful of women police constables appointed in 1958 and later rose to become the first female Senior Superintendent of Police (SSP) in 1999. She served both within and outside Colombo, including at the Criminal Investigation Department and the Police Field Force Headquarters, where she eventually headed the Children and Women's Bureau. Kusuma Devendra turned mid-life to the scholarly study of Buddhism. In 1996, while researching for her doctorate and in the face of considerable opposition, she was ordained as a *bhikkuni*, thereby reviving a Buddhist order of nuns in Sri Lanka after many centuries.

The pages of this book recount a host of "firsts", including many instances when one of these fourteen pioneering women was the first female to reach a milestone in her career. These observations are based on personal recollection, and it was not always possible to confirm such recollection by reference to historical documentation or data. It is easily recognised, however, that these exceptional women are pathbreakers in their chosen fields. Thanks to their determination, as well as countless others like them in Sri Lanka's ancient and contemporary history, Sri Lanka is a more inclusive and meritocratic society. We no longer conceive of a country in which only men compete, direct, perform, write, create, manage, educate, heal, advocate, build, police, and minister. Today, young women take on all these roles, sometimes to the same or greater extent than their male counterparts. Moreover, they are likely to hail from a wider range of socio-economic backgrounds than the earliest female pioneers.

Of course, much more remains to be done. There are still few women who enter fields like engineering, the security forces, and religious orders, and women remain scarce in the highest reaches of most occupations. A career in perhaps the most powerful domain of all – national politics – is a particularly formidable aspiration for women. Although half a century has elapsed since Mrs Bandaranaike took office, the promise of her legacy for women in politics is far from being realised. Today, men comprise 95% of elected members of Sri Lanka's parliament, making the percentage of female parliamentarians the lowest in South Asia and one of the lowest in the world. Yet the extraordinary vision and feats of the pioneers profiled in this book remind us that women need not be daunted.

A remarkable theme in the lives of these distinguished women is that each accomplished a great deal *outside* their regular occupations. Indeed, as the careers of Kumari Jayawardena and Jezima Ismail show, their achievements often span multiple fields. Bhikkuni Kusuma was a teacher and scholar of science, while Stella de Silva, Vajira Dias and K.G. Badra all taught their respective disciplines. Mallika Hemachandra is a culinary expert and former caterer. Maureen Seneviratne is a gifted musician, Premala Sivaprakasapillai Sivasegaram a published author and talented dancer, and Barbara Sansoni wrote in multiple genres. Premila Diwakara competed in international athletics meets, while Sumitra Peries served as Sri Lanka's delegate to UNESCO and its ambassador to France and Spain. Anne Abayasekara is a trained family counsellor, and Rohini Nanayakkara served on the Presidential task force to rebuild the country following the devastating tsunami in 2004.

There are two other pioneer women of this generation whom we wish to specifically mention here, and to whom this book is dedicated. The first is Irene Panditaratne (née Jayawardena) who was born in Hakgala in 1912 and passed away in 2009, during the writing of this book. She was a designer, creator and supplier of batiks, who was among the first to develop this now popular craft in Sri Lanka when she began her batik business in Mount Lavinia in the late 1950s. Moreover, she was an immensely caring mother-in-law and grandmother to the authors of this book. We miss her greatly.

This book is also dedicated to Susima Karunaratne (née Gooneratne) who was born in Panadura in 1924 and now resides in Colombo. Widowed at the age of 39, she raised her four children alone, financing their education and other needs with earnings from a plantation and later, as a real estate agent. This was a highly unusual livelihood for women of that time – requiring her to transport herself alone to show property around the country – and she was thus a pioneering personality in her own right. To the authors, she has been a doting mother and grandmother, and we are delighted that she can see our work to fruition.

We are very thankful for the love, commitment and active support of others in our family, most importantly of Daman Panditaratne, Dumith Fernando, and Rehan Panditaratne. They have sustained and championed us, in ways large and small, including in the writing of this volume. Yohan Fernando and Amar Fernando were admirably tolerant of the time spent on this project, providing endless affection and lovable distraction in the process. There are many others who contributed specifically to this book, by, for example, introducing us to the eminent women we profiled, and by providing valuable advice about its publication. We deeply appreciate their wisdom and assistance.

Naturally, we express our most heartfelt appreciation to the fourteen central figures of this book who generously accepted our invitation to be part of this project. Each of them welcomed us into their homes, their workplaces, and their memories, patiently detailing and clarifying their life stories with diligence and good humour. Our hope is that this book serves as a lasting tribute to their manifold achievements and contributions, a gentle reminder of what we owe to their spirit and fortitude, and an inspiration for generations to come.

Dinusha Panditaratne &
Shalini Panditaratne

Anne Abayasekara at her desk in her room in the Editorial Dept. of The Associated Newspapers of Ceylon Ltd. (ANCL), at Lake House, Colombo, 1947

Anne Abayasekara
Journalist

Most Sri Lankans would have come across at least one article by Anne Abayasekara (née Ameresekere) in a local newspaper or magazine. A well-known journalist, Anne's career spans a remarkable sixty-six years, traversing decades of social, cultural, and political change. Having begun in 1943 on what was then the *Ceylon Daily News* (CDN), Anne continues to write regularly as a freelance journalist until the present day. She credits her long and successful career as much to the strong influence of her family and school in her formative years as to her enduring love of writing.

Anne's mother Frances (née Jayewardene) was a very able woman, born to parents who owned estates in the village of Madampe and outlying areas in the Chilaw district. When Frances was a girl, Anne's maternal grandparents moved to Colombo to further their children's education, and took a house in the then fashionable residential quarters of Grandpass. Her mother attended Pettah Girls' High School, Grandpass (forerunner to Methodist College, Colombo), where she excelled at her studies. Unfortunately, shortly before her Junior Cambridge examination, Frances' younger brother passed away at the tender age of seven. Devastated by this untimely death, Anne's grandmother moved back to Madampe, taking Frances along and thus ending her youthful dreams and aspirations.

Anne believes that her mother never overcame her disappointment and regret that she could not complete her education. When Frances later married and had children of her own – a son named Daniel (called Ira), followed four years later by Anne – she was determined to give them the best education she could. Perhaps, being foiled in fulfilling her academic ambitions allowed her mother time to develop other talents. Anne remembers her mother as excelling in every household art and skill. Anne herself loathed cooking and sewing and gratefully recalls that she was never forced to learn the "womanly" crafts which seemed to come naturally to her mother, who only encouraged Anne to study. Having given her children every opportunity and support throughout their respective careers, Frances died at the age of 93 while living with Anne.

It was during the depression years in the 1930s that Anne began schooling at Ladies'

College, Colombo, where her early years were in the college hostel. Throughout the country, people experienced hardships and Anne's family too was thrust into a difficult period when the price of coconut slumped to a new low of eight rupees per thousand. When her parents reluctantly informed the Principal, Miss Gwen Opie, that their circumstances left them no choice other than to remove Anne from Ladies' College, Miss Opie stepped in with the magnanimous gesture of an indefinite scholarship, enabling Anne to continue at school. When she was ten years old, her parents decided to move to Colombo so that she and her brother Ira could reside with them, rather than in boarding facilities.

Throughout school, Anne enjoyed English, and in particular, the art of writing. It was in the third form that Anne became aware of her ability to write. She placed first in English that year and continued to perform well in the subject. Her teacher in the third form, Miss Harriet de Kretser, was very encouraging and Anne recalls that she won a newspaper essay competition during the school holidays that year. Her teacher the following year, an Englishwoman by the name of Miss Paramour, was equally supportive. By this time, Anne was aware that she had a gift for writing. Such talent did not stop in the family with Anne, for her brother Ira also showed a passion for writing from a young age.

Both siblings wrote for their respective school publications, and Anne was also the editor of her school magazine. During Anne's years at school, the *CDN* and *Sunday Observer* newspapers published youth pages. She and Ira began writing prolifically and their articles would often appear on these pages. Anne proceeded to complete the Senior Cambridge examination, with distinctions in English Language and Literature.

Although she would have loved to proceed to university, Anne recognised that she needed to be employed, as she knew her parents would have found it difficult to support her through a tertiary education. From an early age, she had dreamt of joining the Associated Newspapers of Ceylon Ltd – more commonly known as Lake House (the company's headquarters) – which at the time was regarded as the most successful publishing house in Sri Lanka. The Chairman and Managing Director of Lake House, Mr D.R. Wijewardena, the publishing icon known to all simply as "D.R.", was always on the lookout for fresh talent for his newspapers and it so happened that one day, he called Anne's brother Ira for an interview at his residence at Braybrooke Place in Colombo. Upon his return home from the interview, Ira smiled at Anne and said, "I think I spoke more about you than myself. Mr Wijewardena wants you to come for an interview."

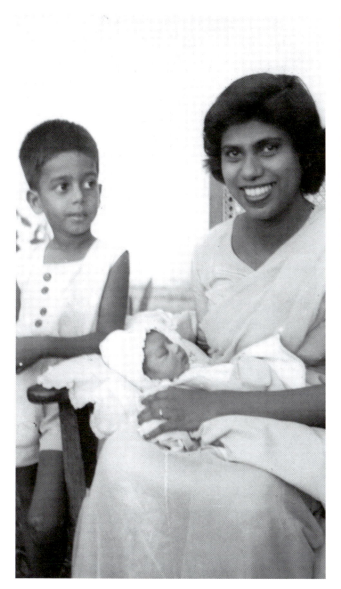 

Anne with her newborn third child (second son), Ranjan, whose elder brother, Rohan, stands by, May 1951

Earle and Anne Abayasekara, outside their home in Wellawatte, 1997

Anne was stunned, and delighted, to hear this unexpected news. She was only seventeen and just out of school. So it was with some trepidation that she approached D.R.'s imposing residence for her interview. But the great man soon put her at ease and Anne told him of her aspiration to work at a Lake House newspaper. D.R. explained to Anne that due to the severe rationing of newsprint in wartime conditions, the women's pages had been temporarily suspended. (At the time, female reporters were only considered for positions to cover the women's pages and not for other reporting in the Editorial Section.) He offered Anne a clerical position in the General Office until conditions normalised, at which point she could expect to move to the Editorial Section.

In January 1943, Anne and Ira went to Lake House to receive their Letters of Appointment. She thinks she must have looked a strange sight, clad in her school uniform and ankle length socks, and her hair in two little plaits! Nevertheless, she must have made a favourable impression on the man who handed her the Letter of Appointment. He was the company's Assistant Secretary, Mr Earle Abayasekara, whom she would marry three years later! On 1 February 1943, two months shy of her eighteenth birthday, Anne entered the portals of the great newspaper institution to commence her first employment.

Before long, however, Anne became bored with the clerical work in the General Office. Realising her potential and her love for writing, D.R. took a personal interest in her career development and did whatever possible under the circumstances to maintain her love for writing. He requested the Editorial Section to give her passes to the cinema so that she could write film reviews. Despite a busy schedule, he found time to give her business and literary magazines, to read as well as to test her broader skills. "I was a duffer at arithmetic. A kind senior colleague would help me out and I think Mr Wijewardene soon realised I was not cut out for numbers!" says Anne. Learning of Anne's tedium in the General Office, D.R. arranged for her to be transferred to the more interesting Secretary's Department, where she came directly under the supervision of Earle Abayasekara.

Anne's happy recollections of Lake House are not confined to memories of her working life there. Not long after commencing employment, Anne and Earle fell in love. "It was a gradual process," she describes. When they decided to get married, Anne tendered her resignation to the Company Secretary, Mr P.C.A. Nelson, due to a company rule that a husband and wife could not work in the same department. She recalls that Mr Nelson read the letter and appeared quite puzzled by it. "But why?" he asked Anne, and when she replied that she was to be married, he pressed her by inquiring, "To whom?" "His mouth fell open," describes Anne, when she named the young man sitting at a desk only a few paces away. Anne and Earle had managed to keep their romance so secret that no one in the office had even suspected it! They were eventually married on 18 March 1946.

A year later, Lake House resumed the women's pages in their newspapers. Anne's initial excitement upon hearing this turned to disappointment when she learned that Leela Shukla, an Indian who was in the country at the time with her husband, was appointed to head the section. Fortunately for Anne, the Shuklas returned to India after a few months, paving the way for D.R. to offer Anne the post of editor of the women's pages of both the *CDN* and the *Sunday Observer*, from January 1947. Anne was, of course, elated. It was a challenging role for a 22 year old, for there were three full pages in the *CDN* and a page in the *Sunday Observer*, plus the twice-weekly women's sections in the *Evening Observer*. She was the first Sri Lankan woman to head the women's pages and the only female in the Editorial Section at the time. Anne recounts that she basically had to "learn on the job" but was ably guided and supported by her sub-editors. She had the privilege of working with two outstanding newspaper editors, Mr H.A.J. Hulugalle of the *CDN* and Mr H.D. Jansz of the *Observer*, both of whom were extraordinarily kind and encouraging to the 'new girl' around.

Anne learnt quickly, in a busy environment where there were always events to be covered and personalities to be interviewed. She remembers being slightly taken aback when D.R. sent for her one day and asked her to write on the fashions at the Robert's Cup and Governor's Cup, two major horse racing events at the time, which were held in August. She had to purchase new outfits herself to attend these grand events! Two very fashion-conscious women of the time who stand out in Anne's memory are Yvonne Toussaint (later Mrs Gulamhusein) and Frances Smith, each of whom were regularly featured in her fashion pages, dressed in their own individual and very contrasting styles.

In 1948, Sita Jayawardena, a former classmate of Anne's, joined as editor of the women's pages of the *Sunday Observer*. Anne describes that she and Sita shared an office at the far end of the Editorial Section, adjoining the office of Mr Hulugalle. It certainly was a room with a view for on a clear day, even Adam's Peak was visible. Transport was not a problem since a station wagon was at their disposal to ferry them to interviews together with an accompanying photographer, enabling a rapid turnaround of reports. They were each required

Anne seated on the steps leading to Arcadia Cottage, Diyatalawa, a favourite holiday haunt of the family, 1953

Anne while travelling abroad

by the management to maintain scrapbooks, which Anne has carefully preserved to this day.

The pages which Anne edited were not confined to matters of fashion, beauty and cookery, although these areas were, of course, given their due place at that time. With three pages to fill in the *CDN* on Mondays, Wednesdays and Saturdays, Anne had to write a great deal. Her work was complemented, however, by valued and regular outside contributors. One of these contributors was Ruth Bagnall, who wrote on child psychology and child-rearing under her maiden name of Ruth Randall. Another was Eileen Hemple, who wrote a delightful series about her family using the nom-de-plume 'Penny Feather'. Other contributors included Mrs Sylvia (E.C.) Fernando, and Winifred Wickramanayake (née Rodrigo) – who was one of the first women to enter Oxford University from Sri Lanka. On Saturdays, Anne compiled a popular feature entitled "Between us Women", which covered matters of general interest to women.

When asked what she regards as the most interesting aspect of her work, Anne immediately and succinctly responds that it is "meeting people". Among the high-profile individuals she interviewed was Sir Ivor Jennings, who was a renowned expert on constitutional law and became the first Vice-Chancellor of the then University of Ceylon. At the time, there were only a few women in university and Anne recounts that she asked him what mark women were likely to make. "They will have a definite contribution to make," replied Sir Ivor. "Give them ten years." In reflecting whether he was right, Anne does not seem to think it panned out quite the way he predicted, as it was only recently that a Sri Lankan university appointed a female Vice-Chancellor.

As editor of the women's pages, Anne interviewed countless women in many different fields, whom she describes as "giants of the past". They include such famous names in Sri Lanka as Cissy Cooray, the first woman senator, and Dr Mary Rutnam, the first woman member of the Colombo Municipal Council – both of whom worked to elevate the status of women in Sri Lanka. To that end, Cissy Cooray and Dr Rutnam – a woman of Canadian origin who married a Sri Lankan – launched the historically well-known *Mahila Samitiya* organisation in Sri Lanka. One of the first women in the Sri Lankan parliament was Florence Senanayake, whom Anne also had the privilege of interviewing. Among women in sports, she featured Irene Williams, a champion athlete who represented Sri Lanka internationally. The extent of someone's perceived status or achievements, however, did not matter to Anne, as she relished interacting with people from all walks of life. She recalls meeting a lady in a village named Morakelle who was probably Sri Lanka's first woman headman. Although some urbanized people may not find the achievements of a female headman to be significant, it was an encounter which Anne immensely enjoyed.

Perhaps the most memorable day in Anne's career was Sri Lanka's Independence Day on 4 February 1948. It is an occasion which she describes as "the most stirring event of my life." Carrying her special pass to the Independence Hall (now known as Independence Square), she entered the hall decorated in *rali palam* (an elaborate paper decoration) where *bera karayas* (drummers) were assembled in full force to greet the large number of dignitaries, envisaging the dawn of a new and glorious era for Sri Lanka.

She recalls the inspiring speeches delivered by S.W.R.D. Bandaranaike and J.R. Jayawardene, who would both become future leaders of the country. There was an evening ball which followed at the Governor-General's official residence, Queen's House, which was itself a night to remember. Among the other celebratory functions was a glittering evening party hosted by the Prime Minister D.S. Senanayake and Mrs Senanayake on the colourfully illuminated lawns of the official residence, Temple Trees. What saddens Anne today, however, is that the brave new Sri Lanka that she and countless others expected did not materialise.

A few years later, Anne had the novel and interesting experience of covering a meeting in the Town Hall organised by the *Eksath Kantha Peramuna* (United Women's Front), a women's feminist socialist group founded in 1948 and spearheaded by Doreen Wickramasinghe and Wimala Wijewardene. The meeting attracted an enormous gathering of women from around the country. So eloquent and impressive were some of the speakers that Anne entitled her feature about the event "Voice of Woman Demands to be Heard."

Although Anne's work did not necessitate overseas travel, there was an international dimension to her work in meeting and interviewing foreign dignitaries and VIPs, which sometimes entailed boarding a visiting cruise liner. She was often accompanied in this work by Sita, making such interviews all the more enjoyable. One especially celebrated woman whom they were both delighted to meet was Indira Gandhi, on the occasion that she accompanied her father Jawaharlal Nehru to Sri Lanka. When Anne interviewed her at Queen's House, it was merely as the daughter of India's Prime Minister; never did she imagine that Indira herself would one day be Prime Minister of India. Anne also recalls covering the conference of Commonwealth Foreign Ministers which was held in Colombo in

1950. She had the unusual opportunity to meet and converse with the wives of these ministers – some of whom had never previously travelled to the East, let alone to Sri Lanka.

Anne combined her career as a journalist with a rich and lively family life. She and Earle welcomed the first of their seven children in 1949. They were lucky to have Anne's parents living with them when she resumed work after three months' maternity leave. Although flexible working hours were uncommon in those days, the nature of her job made it possible to be somewhat adaptable in her daily routine. Moreover, she was fortunate to have a car, a driver, and other domestic help to assist with daily activities and chores. Earle was a great strength and support to her and she was able to keep writing, despite what she jokingly refers to as "the bad habit of reproducing!"

After Anne gave birth to her second child, it became necessary to have someone deputise for her at Lake House. She selected Charmaine Poulier, another young woman just out of school, who would later achieve eminence elsewhere in quite a different capacity. "None of us foresaw that Charmaine (who later married Reuben Solomon), would achieve fame and fortune in Australia as the author of innumerable cookbooks," remarks Anne, referring to the now widely-known Charmaine Solomon whose recipes and cooking products feature in print, television, and stores around the globe.

In reflecting on her pioneering role as a female journalist, Anne does not feel that being a woman posed a special set of challenges, although the fact that she only covered women's issues may have helped in this regard. She was always pleased to see more women join the Editorial Section as the years went by. One of them was yet another diffident school leaver by the name of Maureen Milhuisen, who would later become the highly regarded author Maureen Seneviratne. Around 1951, Ranji Handy joined the organisation and broke new ground as the first woman journalist in general reporting, with coverage extending to parliamentary affairs.

Anne resigned from Lake House following the birth of her third child. "The great thing about journalism," she explains, "is that even if you give up working in an office, you need never stop writing and can work as a freelance writer for as long as you wish." She proved this fact amply by her regular contributions to the Sunday Times during the 1960s. By then an experienced mother, she wrote mainly about bringing up her children, in a feature aptly titled "Life with the Seven". She frequently contributed to several other newspapers and magazines throughout her long career, including the English-language weekly for women *Lanka Woman* from its inception in

1984 (when it was founded and edited by the late Clare Senewiratne) until 2004. In 1989, when the Zonta Club of Colombo launched its now famous Woman of Achievement Awards, Anne was honoured to receive an award for journalism.

Few are aware that Anne's work extends beyond the realm of writing. She trained to be a family counsellor under the Rev. Dr Mervyn Fernando and has engaged in counselling on a voluntary basis for the past 35 years. Anne found this work to be highly satisfying and worthwhile. Besides offering face-to-face counselling, she wrote "The Anne Abayasekara Page for Personal Problems" for *Lanka Woman*, which was popular with readers of all ages and both sexes. In response to the need for sex education among young people, Anne collaborated with Dr Patricia Weerakoon (whom she describes as the country's first qualified sex therapist and who now resides in Australia) in writing a book entitled *Love, Sex and Marriage* – intended especially for Sri Lankan readers and marketed accordingly at an affordable price. The book was commissioned by the Wesley Press, which published it in the 1980s and later translated the volume into Sinhala and Tamil editions.

When considering the position of female journalists in Sri Lanka today, Anne remarks that Sri Lankan women have more than proved themselves in the field. They are capable of tackling any topic and now seem to outnumber their male colleagues. She notes that one difference between then and now "is the job is not as cushy as in those days," as she smilingly recollects the comfortable rides in the chauffeur-driven company car! She points out that nowadays both men and women journalists often need to arrange their own transport and many have to travel considerable distances by bus.

Anne is blissfully content with her long and illustrious career, summarising it simply as a "very rewarding and fulfilling experience." A collection of many of her articles about her family, which have appeared in a variety of newspapers and magazines over the years, was published in 2005 by Vijitha Yapa Publications under the exuberant title *Hurrah! For Large Families* and with a fittingly delightful cover design by the well-known author-illustrator, Sybil Wettasinghe. Of Anne's many fine attributes, perhaps the most inspiring to others is her unwaveringly positive attitude. Though she feels that she should slow down at her age, she has not ceased to write, thereby continuing a lifelong endeavour that has provided so much enjoyment to her, and undoubtedly, to her multitude of readers.

Barbara Sansoni at the opening of her exhibition at the Ceylon Tea Centre, London, July 1966

Barbara Sansoni
Artist & Designer

"Instead of writing, I drew. I drew everything. If I wanted to write a letter, I drew. It was easier than writing," says Barbara Sansoni, the well-known artist who is renowned for her creativity in designing colourful, hand-woven textiles made in Sri Lanka. The depth of her talent is evident the moment one steps into her vibrant and popular gallery, Barefoot, a distinctive building on Colombo's busy Galle Road in Bambalapitiya. Barefoot exhibits a colourful, eye-catching range of handwork ranging from woven fabric, clothes, soft-toys and linen, to books, artwork and much more.

Hailing from her mother's Dutch Burgher lineage, Barbara links her flair for woven design to "a great culture of love of textiles in the Netherlands," where in days when there was no convenient form of heating, textiles were used as a mode of insulation. People turned to carpets, curtains and clothing to keep them warm, such necessities becoming art forms over the years.

Born in 1928 in Kandy, Barbara was fortunate to experience life in many parts of Ceylon during her childhood, as a result of her father, R.Y. Daniel of the Ceylon Civil Service, being transferred from one town to another in his capacity as Assistant Government Agent or Government Agent. Batticaloa, Mannar, Matara, Kurunegala and Kandy are some of the towns with which the young Barbara became acquainted during her early years. The eighteen months or so spent in the Assistant Government Agent's bungalow in Browns Hill, Matara from 1939 – the year World War II broke out – were particularly special to Barbara. "I loved Matara, going about in buggy carts and attending music lessons at Mrs Felsinger's charming house in the Fort. And all those children's birthday parties with patties and rainbow sandwiches," she reminisces fondly – "with fireworks afterwards".

Barbara remembers her mother Bertha as a kind and wonderfully socially-minded woman, who was a great supporter of the Sisters of the Good Shepherd in Sri Lanka. Bertha Daniel worked with the nuns of St Anthony's Convent in Batticaloa in their efforts making children's clothes and linen, thus helping women who were in the care of the nuns to earn a home-based income and learn a hand skill. Barbara holds nostalgic memories of the beautiful white, embroidered and lace-edged clothes made by these women, which she often wore as a child.

Barbara's maternal grandmother Mrs Ethel van Langenberg, whose family came to Sri Lanka in the early 17th century from Holland – now the Netherlands – was herself a van der Straaten, a family from Bruges, in the Flanders region of Belgium. Mrs van Langenberg and her daughters helped set up the Colombo Ladies League, where exquisite linen, lacework and white embroidery are designed and made even today, helping rural women who cannot leave home to make a living, and Sri Lanka to preserve these wonderful skills of its cottage industries. One of Barbara's maternal uncles, Arthur van Langenberg, an unforgettable pianist was an actor and producer and a prominent theatrical personality in Sri Lanka. With this rich artistic heritage, it is not surprising that creativity comes so naturally to Barbara and indeed, she considers herself lucky to have been born into such a family.

About eight years ago, Barbara's present husband – Dr Ronald Lewcock – arranged for them to visit the picturesque city of Bruges. Barbara was absorbing the beautiful architecture of the city's cathedral, when she quite unexpectedly stumbled upon a marble panel inscribed with the van der Straaten family details. "I felt that my grandmother was with me, and it was as if we had just made a bridge over three centuries!" she says delightedly, recalling this remarkable moment. And then, crossing a canal bridge to find nuns of St Anthony's organizing sewing and lace making – she was home!

One of five children in her family, Barbara's parents sent her to the Presentation Convent in Kodaikanal, India, at the tender age of six and a half. She remained there for most of her schooling, returning to Ceylon only for her final year of secondary school. Despite having the company of a brother and sister who were also boarded there, being away from home was not easy for the little Barbara, especially since she could go home only once a year. However, the years she spent in the beautiful hill country of Southern India kindled a deep appreciation of the area's captivating landscape and this early encounter with such natural splendour inspired her artistic inclinations. "I have beautiful memories of my days there and of having a marvellous education. I was very happy, although it was tough being away from home so early. It was, after all, a young age to be independent," she notes.

Being dyslexic, the nuns sent her to Dr Maria Montessori who after a week gave her the best direction of her life. "If you can't write, draw it," she advised firmly. "But history? Arithmetic?" "Draw it," – said Dr Maria Montessori, and Barbara was to remember her well when first confronted by designing for warp and weft, no curves, her creativity stimulated by colour.

She had art lessons from several dedicated

teachers during her youth, including Mr J.D. Perera and Professor Amarasinghe, all of whom she recalls with great affection. After completing her final school year in 1945 at St Bridget's Convent in Colombo, she was able to devote herself more fully to what she loved doing best and in 1947, she sailed to England on the Atlantis to pursue a five-year Diploma in Art at the Regent Street London Polytechnic (now the Chelsea School of Art). Barbara painted and drew using all media. Initially, she used pencils and later experimented with pen and ink. She found crayon and watercolours tedious because the paper had to be dunked and stretched; it was easier to use colours that were quick-drying. "I enjoyed acrylics and oils but what I liked best was my pen," says Barbara.

She learnt much about art over the years, including about the history of art and architecture, old manuscript writing, and sculpture. One of her sculptures, Figure of the Risen Christ, was commissioned for the chapel of the Good Shepherd Convent, Bandarawela in 1981 by Ulrik Plesner (a Danish architect who was in Sri Lanka) and Geoffrey Bawa. The cast of this six foot slab is still in her house in Colombo. In fact, Barbara very much enjoyed sculpting and regrets not having kept up with it. She gave it up because clay was heavy, and needed a lot of attention to be kept pliable and not too dry.

In 1952, the year following her return from England to Sri Lanka, Barbara married her first husband, the sportsman Hildon Sansoni. "My parents were horrified and everyone was shocked because he was a divorcé and twice my age. But I had a wonderful old time!" remembers Barbara. Although Barbara reckons she was not athletic and did not have much in common with Hildon's enthusiasm for sport, she would accompany him to sporting events and use the time to sketch, draw or embroider.

Barbara and Hildon hardly spent any time in Colombo, preferring instead adventure in the jungles of Yala and Wilpattu, swimming and sailing in Trincomalee harbour, or staying with friends upcountry. They were constantly by the water, in the mountains, or amongst wild animals and birds, experiencing a life close to nature. It was only midweek that any time was spent in Colombo, where they would be drawn to the music and dancing at the Galle Face Hotel. "It was," she reminisces, "an absolutely glorious and joyous time, even though I had to make a new life, not having lived in Colombo – apart from the year I attended St Bridget's Convent – and not having many friends there." Gradually though, she became acquainted with other well known artists and architects, such as Geoffrey Bawa, Ulrik Plesner, Nihal Fernando and Laki Senanayake – all exceptionally creative individuals who became a close-knit artistic group over the years, meeting frequently at the Arts Centre Club.

Barbara grew up surrounded by the beauty of lace and cloth. Yet it was not until she was married to Hildon and had two sons that she became involved in weaving. It began in 1958 when she was asked by her friend, Mother of Good Counsel, Provincial of the Good Shepherd nuns, to help start hand-weaving as a way of developing the intelligence of young women placed in her care who had no education whatsoever, in line with Maria Montessori's philosophy. It would also provide a livelihood for the young women in the care of the nuns at the Nayakakande Convent in Hendala when they left their care. This led to the founding of the present work in 1960, which Barbara managed single-handedly, attending to all aspects of the operation from purchasing the raw materials to designing and selling. Originally named Provincial Handlooms to honour Mother Provincial, the project's name was later changed to Barefoot, a name signifying being 'in touch with the earth'.

The art of handloom provided Barbara with the perfect opportunity not only to design, but also to delve ever deeper into the exploration of colour. Barbara learnt that bright colours – for which Barefoot designs are famous – help people feel happier, as colours are known to release endorphins from the brain and be naturally attractive to people. She explains that colour, especially multi-colour, stimulates the creative brain to the extent that a weaver can weave a complex multi-colour check design in half the time it would take to weave a plain cloth. Hence plain white textile takes the longest to weave; the brain is bored with no problems to solve which is why machine mass production has ill-effects on it.

Barbara views handlooms as an evolution of skills, which began with stone-age people weaving their fences from natural material and progressed to the weaving of baskets, mats and cloth. Every thread on a loom that makes up a material – which may end up as a colourful bale of cloth, or a sarong (traditionally worn by Sri Lankan men but in more recent times also worn by women), or even a stuffed toy – is done by hand and of the same tension. "It is like performing an opera. Our symphony is designing and weaving; there is a composer, and a conductor who brings the composer's music to being," explains Barbara.

Barbara and Hildon's sons, Simon and Dominic were reared with the trusted help of two loyal staff; Ekanayake, their major domo, and Jane, the *ayah*. Ekanayake supervised the children's homework and activities in later years and taught them wisdom. The dedication of these two aides freed up time for Barbara and Hildon, allowing them to successfully combine their creative work and leisure activities with the upbringing of their children.

In the early days, Barefoot creations were sold from the couple's home on Anderson Road, Bambalapitiya. Back then, it was a rather casual operation. Ekanayake doubled up as the sales assistant whilst Hildon slipped into a client relations role, greeting customers and offering them refreshments that included *pol sambol* sandwiches, and the 'Sansoni Cocktail' – a unique combination of lime and arrack, enjoyed by many!

After Hildon's death in 1979, Barbara was fortunate to receive advice and assistance from many people. She is especially grateful to Justice Vanam Rajaratnam, who was a great source of strength and comfort to her in those trying times and with advice from his many distinguished friends made the project into a real company. He played a pivotal role in the procurement of the present landmark Barefoot building on the Galle Road and holds the distinction of being Barefoot's first Chairman.

Barbara's present husband was formerly a Fellow at Cambridge and then the Aga Khan Professor of Architecture at the Massachusetts Institute of Technology, before becoming a Professor of Architecture at the Georgia Institute of Technology in the United States. "Ronald retired from there just before his seventy-eighth birthday," she says, "but he is now an Honorary Professor at the University of Queensland in Australia, and still a member of Clare Hall, Cambridge." Barbara has known Ronald since January 1969, when he looked her up because he admired her drawings while on a visit to Sri Lanka to study colonial architecture. After marrying Ronald in 1981, Barbara shuttled between Cambridge, England, Europe, the US, Australia and Sri Lanka. Barbara observes with a contented smile that she has been very happy in both her marriages.

Even after forty five long years with Barefoot and despite her constant travel leading to extended periods overseas, Barbara remained until she was eighty years old, actively engaged as Barefoot's Chief Designer. She entrusted the management of Barefoot to her younger son Dominic, a Fine Arts graduate and photographer, and the very capable Upul Gunatunge. Barbara, Dominic, and Barbara's elder son Simon are all Directors of the company.

Barbara's works have graced many and varied environments. She has exhibited her paintings, woven wall hangings, textiles and panels in numerous exhibitions in Asia, Europe and the United States. Her overseas exhibitions date as far back as 1966, when her drawings and woven

Weaving by Barbara Sansoni: 'Australian Gum'

Artwork by Barbara Sansoni: 'Rice Bins at Embekke'

panels were displayed at the erstwhile Ceylon Tea Centre in London. Her woven fabric has been used as curtains or panels at some of Sri Lanka's most beautiful hotels, including the Bentota Beach Hotel. She has won many accolades in recognition of her contribution and exceptional creative abilities. The prestigious J.D. Rockefeller III Travel Award in 1970 – which enabled her to study craft and folk art for two years in fourteen countries – and a stint in the West Indies as an ILO (International Labour Organisation) craft advisor from 1974 to 1975, are just two examples of this external recognition. In 2001, Barbara delivered a talk at Harvard University about a group of pioneers in contemporary design working in Sri Lanka, the best known being Ena de Silva and her talented entourage, who produce original batiks of international fame.

Barbara's interests are not confined to art and weaving. She is a woman with a deep sense of appreciation of Sri Lanka's rich heritage who is passionate about traditional hand-made houses, the tradition of good furniture makers in Moratuwa and Indian Ocean fishing boats such as the outrigger catamaran. She has great respect for the artisans and craftspeople of Sri Lanka and recalls with deep emotion a fisherman whom she only knew by the name of Joseph, for his simple but effective work, including a clay bin he had built for grain storage. "It is the carpenters, bricklayers, roof layers and the like who really solve problems. Even without a formal education, they have the intellect to craft and to build fine works of art, using their hands and brains and no computers. These are the people to be admired," she says. She holds in esteem the simple cadjan huts made from coconut branches which are constructed without nails, hand-baked clay roof tiles, and the concept of a *meda midula* (a small garden in the centre of the house) and laments that such practical, low-cost concepts – which are ideally suited for Sri Lanka's hot and humid climate – are becoming a rarity today.

A multi-talented individual, Barbara is also a keen writer. As a freelance journalist in the 1950s and 60s, she discovered and drew a house every week for a column in the *Daily Mirror* called "Collecting Old Buildings", as part of a drive to prevent historic buildings from being destroyed. On her weekend visits by foot to various buildings, she would often be accompanied by architecture students, including Ismeth Raheem, Laki Senanayake and others, who measured the buildings under the direction of Ulrik Plesner, while Barbara would draw the perspectives. Her drawings appear in *Viharas and Verandas* and *The Architecture of an Island*, books written by her husband Ronald (the latter in collaboration with Laki Senanayake). In addition, she has written and illustrated a delightful children's book called

Missy Fu and Tikkiri Banda. Also a lover of poetry, she has published a book of light verse and drawings of island faces named *Press with the Toes in the Grass*.

So what was it like to achieve what she did in the context of being a woman? "I never encountered the slightest difficulty being a woman," says Barbara. "In fact, everything I have achieved is owed to men. Men have always been encouraging and helpful. Even the politicians were a delight to work with, from Dudley Senanayake to N.M. Perera to W. Dahanayake," she adds, recalling the challenging period in the 1960s when dyes and yarn were subject to rations and quotas and she was compelled to seek their influence to secure raw materials. In keeping with her values, she attired herself in the traditional 'cloth and jacket' and tied her hair in a bun, undoubtedly making quite a favourable impression when she met with these political leaders!

She remembers one day, in that era, when she received a batch of blotchy, government-dyed yarn. Facing adversity in her usual forthright manner, she decided to raise the matter with none other than the Prime Minister at the time, Dudley Senanayake. Armed with the blotchy bales and a letter addressed to him, she drove to his residence. His personal aide, Carolis, opened the door, and upon hearing her complaint, had a wise solution to offer in the temporary absence of the Prime Minister. "It is best to leave the letter and the bales on Master's bed. He will surely see them," he said. And indeed, upon returning home and seeing the poor quality yarn, the Prime Minister took immediate action, resulting in a vastly improved product.

She also recalls some valuable advice she received from an American gentleman, at a time when the Sansonis' Anderson Road home served as Barefoot's retail outlet and was not doing well financially. "You must advertise," counselled the American. "All you need is half an inch in a daily paper stating 'We are still here. We are still making. Please come and see us'. That was what Henry Ford forgot to do. Thinking he was famous, he did not advertise which lost him his first place as the manufacturer of motor cars." Barbara followed his advice putting two or three lines of verse in the personal column of the *Daily Mirror* and, true to his words, Barefoot reaped the benefits.

Barbara has made an exceptional contribution to Sri Lanka, especially towards uplifting rural women. She facilitated an alternative to mainstream education, developing in them a lifelong skill, and for some, the confidence to embark on their own ventures. As a felicitation for her service to the Sri Lankan handloom industry, "How can it be so right yet,

Artwork by Barbara Sansoni: 'Residency, Matale'

Sarong?" an exhibition on weaving in abstract form displaying beautifully designed *reddhas*, was held at Barefoot in December 2004.

Barbara has remained stoically true to her principles of producing by hand, and keeping factories and machines at bay. Her unceasing efforts to preserve one of Sri Lanka's greatest crafts are underpinned by her amazing determination to live out her values and by the desire for Barefoot to be seen not as a business, but as an enormously fun creative house that helps sustain hundreds of lives. With a simple philosophy very much the same as when it began, "Barefoot," she observes, "is in effect, a continuation of what my mother and grandmother did."

Bhikkuni Kusuma at her ordination, Sarnath, India, 1996

Bhikkuni Kusuma
Buddhist Nun

As once famously remarked, taking the road "less traveled by" can make all the difference. These inspiring words fittingly describe the life of Kusuma Devendra, who has traversed a path diverging from conventional values and choices. After training and working as a science teacher, which itself was unusual for a woman born in the 1920s, Kusuma gradually immersed herself in a greater spiritual calling. She eventually became a *bhikkuni* (ordained Buddhist nun) in 1996, and now presides at a retreat and meditation centre near Gonapola, Horana, in the Kalutara District.

Born in 1929 in the town of Kolonnawa, on the outskirts of Colombo, Kusuma was the third of five children of D.C. Gunawardene and his wife Emelia. During her parents' youth, Sri Lanka experienced a renaissance of Buddhism under the influence of Anagarika Dharmapala and in this era, both her mother and father had become firm Buddhists. After their marriage, her parents took up residence in Kolonnawa where D.C. Gunawardene was an engineer in the Public Works Department. The Gunawardenes led a comfortable existence – complete with a car and upstair house – and the young Kusuma and her four siblings grew up happily, wanting for nothing.

Kusuma received her primary education at Ananda Balika, a school for girls in Colombo, and her secondary education at the illustrious Ananda College, where she was one of the few female students in her class. Like many of her classmates, Kusuma aspired to become a doctor, and was deeply disappointed when she was not granted admission to study medicine at university. She recalls that she gained the necessary examination marks but did not pass the entrance interview – this being an era when it was still common to look unfavourably upon female applicants. It was at this point that Kusuma decided to become a teacher, since it was one of the few professions open to an academically capable girl. She entered the Teacher Training College in Maharagama. There she received specialist instruction in biology and chemistry, which qualified her to teach science to secondary school students.

Kusuma observes that her mother's "enlightened" attitudes facilitated her tertiary education. Although it was common practice for girls like Kusuma to marry soon after completing secondary school, Emelia Gunawardene never pressured Kusuma to do so. On the contrary, she encouraged her daughters to continue studying, aware that she had not had this opportunity herself. Kusuma's elder sister also studied beyond secondary school, reading Indo-Aryan languages at university under such eminent scholars as Professor G.P. Malalasekera.

Upon graduating from college, Kusuma obtained a teaching position at her first alma mater, Ananda Balika. She taught there until her marriage at the age of twenty-six to Asoka Devendra, who was a few years her senior. Theirs was an arranged match, between two like-minded people. Asoka was himself a teacher, specializing in mathematics, and a committed Buddhist. He served in the Department of Education and would later become principal of the Teacher Training College at Maharagama. After their wedding, Kusuma and Asoka moved to Maharagrama, where they began building their house and life together.

Soon after moving to Maharagama in 1956, Kusuma began teaching science at the Government Senior School, a secondary school that was attached to the Teacher Training College. Kusuma had to combine her work as a science teacher with an exceptionally busy family life, since Kusuma and Asoka were blessed with six children born within seven years of each other. Their first child, a daughter, was born in 1957 and was followed by a son, another daughter, their second son and finally, by twin boys.

The Devendras were fortunate to have domestic help and a spacious home for their family. But they otherwise lived simply, in keeping with the fairly modest salaries earned by a teacher and government servant. Kusuma recalls that she woke up early each morning, so that she could cook breakfast and lunch before she left for school, which was fortunately only a few minutes' walk from home. After school, she would rush back to her children to begin her 'second shift', which involved preparing the evening meal as well as sewing all the children's clothes. On weekends, she would boil and wash the laundry, putting them on the roof to dry.

Unsurprisingly, Kusuma's first decade as a mother was consumed by her job and family life, with barely a moment for anything else. As Kusuma describes it, she "was hit against a wall and had to perform!" With six young children, one wonders how Kusuma found the time to prepare her lessons and do her marking – two essential tasks that teachers often perform at home. Kusuma explains frankly that she did not require a great deal of preparation because she was a good teacher who knew her material well. Each year, she usually prepared about forty students for the O-level examinations in bio-science and chemistry, of whom about thirty-eight would succeed. Her students were clearly very keen, since parents would come in and complain to the young Mrs Devendra that their children were studying science to the exclusion of everything else!

Despite the busyness of their daily existence, the Devendras enjoyed a happy family life.

Kusuma recounts her children's view, that although they were not born to a rich family, they enjoyed a carefree and harmonious childhood. Kusuma remembers that the children whiled away their time playing all day – nobody worried about homework and certainly not tuition! Kusuma's parents and in-laws did not live nearby, nor did her sisters and brothers, so they were a close-knit nuclear family who relied on each other for companionship.

This self-contained existence was unexpectedly altered in 1969 when, after a dozen years teaching science, Kusuma was presented with a novel and adventurous opportunity. She won a scholarship to pursue a master's degree in molecular biology in the United States, based at Ball State University in the state of Indiana. The scholarship was awarded through the Asia Foundation and the National Science Foundation, an agency of the US government that supports research in science and engineering. Kusuma accepted this honour and proceeded to America.

But Kusuma soon became homesick, to the extent that she did not want to complete her course. Her children were still young at the time, ranging from the ages of five to twelve. Although she knew they were in good hands, especially as her mother-in-law had come to stay in her absence, Kusuma missed them terribly. It was these previously unknown feelings of loneliness and isolation that first prompted Kusuma's curiosity about the beginning of life and even more fundamentally, about its meaning. She remembers asking her professors for their views on these profound questions, to which they simply replied that the answers were still unknown and undiscoverable. Ultimately, the homesickness overcame her and Kusuma decided to return home after six months in the US. She had been receiving full marks in her tests, and her professors pleaded with her to stay, but all this was to no avail.

Kusuma was glad to return to Sri Lanka and to her family. Yet a sense of internal disquiet remained, and escalated, within her. After experiencing the superb educational facilities in the US, which included fully-equipped modern laboratories, she found it frustrating to teach science when armed with only a blackboard and perhaps a test tube and some gas. The dissatisfaction she felt soon extended to other aspects of Kusuma's life. She began to feel

(above) Kusuma studying at Ball State University in the U.S.
(right) Bhikkuni Kusuma on a snowmobile

enveloped by the cycle of work and life, including her job and her kids, and saw no escape from this.

Kusuma discussed her feelings with her husband, telling him that she no longer desired to teach science and instead, wished to learn more about Buddhism. It was this spiritual endeavour, Kusuma believed, that would pave the way for her freedom from the confines and trials of daily life. And so in 1971, Kusuma left her teaching position and retired from government service, thereby freeing her time to devote to this mission. Unbeknownst to her, she was setting herself on a path that would ultimately lead her – a quarter of a century later – to becoming an ordained Buddhist nun.

Kusuma's greater learning of Buddhism encompassed different elements, beginning with academic study. In 1972, she enrolled in an arts degree at the University of Sri Jayawardenapura, where she studied Pali, Buddhism, and English. Though she had never formally studied arts subjects before, Kusuma was utterly engrossed. She graduated with excellent results, which led her to obtain a position teaching English at the university. Kusuma eventually spent a decade teaching English at Sri Jayawardenapura, until she retired in 1984 at the age of 55. It is a period she describes as the most fruitful of her life, mainly because the students were so weak in English that they skipped most of their classes, enabling

Kusuma to spend ample time reading about Buddhism!

During the 1970s, while teaching at Sri Jayawardenapura, she met and befriended a well-known Buddhist lady of German origin, known as Ayya Khema. Ayya Khema was initiated as a ten-precept nun in Sri Lanka and was later involved in a nascent movement called *Sakyadhita*, which is now a fully-fledged international association of Buddhist women. The closeness between the two women was such that Ayya Khema began using Kusuma's house as her mailing address. She would come every day to Maharagama to collect her mail, thereby becoming a household figure to Kusuma and her family. The friendship inspired a natural, organic spiritual growth within Kusuma, which complemented her academic study of Buddhism. Kusuma frequently accompanied Ayya Khema around Sri Lanka, translating her talks on Buddhism and meditation from English into Sinhalese. She also began to learn and practise *vipassana* (Buddhist meditation) herself.

Kusuma completed her master's degree in Buddhism and embarked on her first doctorate in the 1980s, both at the University of Sri Jayawardenapura. In 1982, however, Kusuma was struck by a personal tragedy that stirred her far more profoundly and forcefully than anything she had studied or experienced before. It was in this year that she lost her younger daughter Aruni, who passed away from ovarian cancer at the tender age of 21. Kusuma recalls that Aruni was a beautiful girl who, like all her siblings, went to university, where she was an outstanding physics student. It was Aruni's death, Kusuma explains, "that really put me onto the other side." Kusuma began to search more deeply for life's meaning, asking herself, "What is this world offering me?" Though by now she had read the whole *tripitaka* (Buddhist scriptures) in English, Pali, and Sinhala, her knowledge and scholarship no longer seemed enough.

While Kusuma did not consciously aspire to become a nun at this time, she began to learn more about this possibility through her doctoral research, which was on the subject of nuns in Sri Lanka. The dissertation took several years to research and write as she first needed to travel throughout the island, visiting nuns in remote areas. She had the good fortune at the time to meet an American sociologist and professor, Lowell Bloss, who was in Sri Lanka supervising some of his students and whose research also involved meeting Sri Lankan nuns. While accompanying Professor Bloss' small contingent and translating for them from Sinhala to English, Kusuma was able to collect much of her material. Professor Bloss also taught Kusuma how to process this collected data, so that she carried out her research systematically. His informal tutelage was immensely valuable, since Kusuma had trained as a scientist and did not have previous experience with sociological data.

Alas, however, Kusuma was unable to receive her PhD for the resulting dissertation. She submitted it just before the insurrection of the late 1980s, a particularly calamitous period in Sri Lanka's history during which universities were closed. The consideration and progress of the dissertation was greatly delayed, eventually leading to Kusuma abandoning the PhD. Nevertheless, the dissertation remains an important historical record of nuns in Sri Lanka during the early 1980s. It provides an insight into a rarely discussed facet of Sri Lankan religious life, even though – as Kusuma describes – Sri Lankan nuns "have come a long way since then." Recognizing its potential to educate both scholars and lay readers, Kusuma has recently prepared the dissertation for publication.

Aside from not receiving her doctoral degree, Kusuma faced another disappointing aspect of her research. Kusuma had begun to consider joining the clergy but discovered to her dismay that none of the nuns whom she studied was ordained. Rather, they were all so-called 'ten-precept nuns' – that is, religious women who had undertaken to observe certain practices in addition to the usual five precepts followed by lay Buddhists. Kusuma explains that such ten-precept nuns, who have featured in modern Sri Lankan Buddhism for over a century, are essentially still lay persons. They do not wear the robe of monks (which is distinctly coloured and sewn, in a yellow fabric) and do not use the monk's bowl for taking alms. Although ten-precept nuns leave the home, this event is more of an initiation, not an ordination. They do not have *vinaya* (rules of discipline for ordained clergy), and receive neither an income nor an education – since only monks are recognized by the government and are educated in state-funded seminaries.

As Kusuma elaborates, there were ordained nuns in Sri Lanka's ancient history but these bhikkunis disappeared about a millennium ago. It is widely believed that Sanghamitta, the daughter of the Emperor Ashoka, brought the bhikkuni order to Sri Lanka in the 3rd century BC, after which countless women in Sri Lanka became bhikkunis. Kusuma relates that Sri Lankan bhikkunis travelled to China in the 6th century AD to establish a female order there, and from China, bhikkuni orders were later established in other countries where *Mahayana* Buddhism predominated, including in Korea. The female orders continued in such countries, but they did not spread to other seats of *Theravada* Buddhism, such as Burma and Thailand. Thus after the disappearance of bhikkunis in Sri Lanka, there were no ordained nuns in any country where the *Theravada* school prevails.

After studying ten-precept nuns in Sri Lanka, Kusuma resolved not to join this community. She discovered that many women became such nuns under the false assumption that they would be equal to *bhikkus* (ordained Buddhist monks). By the time these women discovered that they were not regarded as such, they had already left their homes and felt compelled to stay, even though they were marginalized from the mainstream and did not receive alms. They would have to beg for food and cook the raw provisions which they received by themselves.

Though certain that she did not want to become a ten-precept nun, Kusuma contemplated becoming an ordained nun if an order of bhikkunis were reestablished in Sri Lanka. Despite the advocacy of the *Sakyadhita* movement and other supporters of female ordination, however, there was no indication that such reestablishment would occur. Around 1989, Kusuma began conducting research for her second doctoral dissertation, which was on *Bhikkuni Vinaya* (rules of discipline for ordained Buddhist nuns). This was evidently an important topic to understand and clarify before any restoration of a bhikkuni order in Sri Lanka. Kusuma spent ten years researching and writing her dissertation and this time was duly rewarded, successfully receiving her PhD from the Buddhist and Pali University of Sri Lanka in 1999.

A critical part of Kusuma's second doctoral research was spent in Frankfurt, Germany, which she visited in 1989 to study *vinaya* under Dr Friedgard Lottermoser, a scholar specializing in this field. As Kusuma discovered and wrote, the disciplinary rules for women are slightly different to those for men; there being (in the

Kusuma ordained, Sarnath, India, 1996

Theravada tradition) 311 rules for ordained nuns and 227 for monks, with 91 rules common to both sexes. Like her first dissertation, this second dissertation is also being prepared for publication. Kusuma explains that she was reluctant to publish her work earlier because the re-emergence of bhikkunis in Sri Lanka is a new and controversial phenomenon. She did, however, translate and publish her English writings into Sinhala. This publication is now regarded as a 'handbook' for Buddhist nuns in Sri Lanka.

The immediate catalyst for Kusuma's own ground-breaking ordination occurred while she was researching for her second doctorate. In this period, she came to know Venerable Vipulasara, a Sri Lankan monk who was then president of the well-regarded Maha Bodhi Society in India. Venerable Vipulasara was supportive of female ordination and suggested to Kusuma that she be ordained, and thereby initiate a bhikkuni order in Sri Lanka. He was well connected to some Korean bhikkus and bhikkunis, many of whom visited Sri Lanka to study. After discussing the matter with them, Venerable Vipulasara informed Kusuma that they were willing to support and ordain Sri Lankan nuns.

At his suggestion, Kusuma travelled to South Korea to research their ordination procedure for bhikkunis. She had previously studied female ordination in the time of the Buddha and in ancient Sri Lanka. Somewhat to her surprise, Kusuma found that the same procedure was still followed by Korean clergy. As she describes it, the procedure for ordaining bhikkunis is a dual one. They are first ordained with nuns and on the same day, they are ordained again with monks (whereas for men, there is no dual ordination since they are ordained only by monks).

Knowing that Kusuma was satisfied with the procedure of ordination, Venerable Vipulasara arranged for a large group of Korean monks and nuns to travel to Sarnath in India, and for ten nuns from Sri Lanka to simultaneously travel there to receive ordination from them. Before this could transpire, however, Venerable Vipulasara came under fire from some monks in Sri Lanka, who criticized him for encouraging female ordination and in particular, what they regarded as '*Mahayana* bhikkunis'. He was in a very delicate position, but Kusuma, realizing that this could be a historical turning point, pleaded with him not to cancel the ordination which she believed "might never otherwise happen". To his credit, Venerable Vipulasara agreed to proceed.

Kusuma too was at a stage of her life in which she felt able to take this bold step. Her children were married and settled, and her husband – being a practicing Buddhist – also understood. So Kusuma simply left home, alone, carrying only a cloth bag with some white clothes. In retrospect, Kusuma feels that she was unconsciously preparing for this role her whole life; from her education in the sciences, to her study of Pali, practice of meditation, and learning Buddhism both at university and under the inspiration of Ayya Khema. Kusuma's journey towards this historic turning point was also undoubtedly precipitated by the aching loss of her daughter, her extensive but ultimately disappointing research on ten-precept nuns, and her decade of enlightening research into the *vinaya* for women.

Joined by nine other women from Sri Lanka, Kusuma travelled to Sarnath, where they were ordained in December 1996. The Korean clergy returned to their country, while the newly-ordained Sri Lankan nuns remained in India for two years to complete their training. They resided there with one Sri Lankan monk, Venerable Devasiri, who trained them in the Pali tradition. When asked why she and the other nuns were not trained in Sri Lanka, Kusuma replies that they dared not! Their ordination was a polemical event which made world news. The headlines in Sri Lanka featured Kusuma as the first ordained nun, exposing her to intense criticism from conservative quarters.

It was at this time that Kusuma's education and experience proved enormously beneficial, enabling her to face criticism with confidence and eloquence. After all, she was an educated woman who had travelled solo abroad and had taught English at university – including to hundreds of monks – so she could readily speak for herself. She also recalls that while she schooled at Ananda College, she was one of a handful of girls in a class of about thirty boys. There she bore the good-natured teasing and banter of her classmates. As she describes it, the experience helped her to be independent and fearless and "not scared of all those fellows put together"!

Her fellow alumni from Ananda College, who went on to become doctors, lawyers and leaders of the community, helped her in other ways too. She remembers that when news of the ordination reached some of her former classmates in England, they chartered a plane and flew to greet her in Sarnath, India. When she later went to Australia, a branch of the alumni association hosted a reception and gave her a standing ovation; it was commented there that the founder of Ananda, Colonel Olcott, would never have believed that a pioneer bhikkuni would have been produced by the college! These were all encouraging gestures that Kusuma greatly appreciated.

After two years in India, Kusuma returned to Sri Lanka with the other bhikkunis who had completed their training. Upon their return, there was again much public and theological discussion about the ordination of women, with some speaking for it and some against. But after all had been said, the discussion subsided. As Kusuma notes, "people had other things to worry about," and she herself kept a low profile. She did not wish to be in the limelight, being satisfied that she had played her part and could now live the spiritual life that she sought. Kusuma estimates that there are now several hundred bhikkunis in Sri Lanka and notes that ordinations are now done locally.

Since becoming a bhikkuni, Kusuma has been based in Sri Lanka but she periodically travels overseas to teach meditation. Regardless of the climate, she always dons her robes. Several of her talks abroad have been published in booklet form. During her travels, she gradually collected small donations to build a Buddhist retreat and meditation centre in Olaboduwa, off Gonapola, south-east of Colombo. She first came here after returning to Sri Lanka from India. She had no place to live at the time and took up residence at a local nunnery, opposite which there was bare land. Kusuma initially bought a small plot of this land on her own, and later obtained an adjoining one and a half acres with a gift from Ayya Khema's Buddha-Haus in Germany. The two-storey meditation centre, dedicated to Ayya Khema and described by Kusuma as the "crowning glory", was completed in 2008.

Kusuma also spends considerable time in Colombo, where she has a room at a temple in Rajagiriya. She regularly sees her daughter, who launders Kusuma's robes and often invites the rest of the family to visit. This way, Kusuma's grandchildren can occasionally enjoy her company! However, only her daughter and second son live in Sri Lanka. Her eldest son tragically died of cancer after she returned from India as a bhikkuni and her twin sons are abroad – one who has a doctorate in mathematics lives in Canada and the other, an honours graduate in mathematics, is in Dubai.

When asked whether she misses her family, including her children and twelve grandchildren, Kusuma replies that while she might miss them, she is too involved with her spiritual life to notice. She is satisfied knowing that she has raised her family and "done everything" in secular life before becoming a bhikkuni, so that there is nothing to revisit and regret. Indeed, Kusuma's life has focused – more than most – on looking forward, preparing not just for this life but with a view to what may lie hereafter.

Jezima Ismail as Chancellor of South Eastern University of Sri Lanka, 2003

Jezima Ismail
Social Activist & Educationist

With her rare blend of grace, wisdom and strength, Jezima Ismail commands deep respect across many segments of Sri Lankan society. Since graduating from the University of Ceylon in 1955, she has worked in fields as diverse as education, human rights, and broadcasting, earning senior positions and distinguished accolades along the way. In the process, she has addressed some of the country's most critical issues, including those related to the development of youth, women's rights, peace and democracy, and inter-faith relations.

Jezima's multi-faceted career and achievements are rooted in the manner of her upbringing. Born in Colombo in 1935, Jezima recalls her parents as loving, intelligent, and progressive individuals. Both of them expected high ethical and educational standards of their three daughters, of whom Jezima was the youngest. When people would comment to her parents that they had no sons and ask who would carry on the family name, Jezima's father would perspicaciously reply that he planned to educate his daughters to be independent and thus had no need of a son.

Jezima's father, Mohamed Thamby Sahid Ahamed, had left his middle-class home in the village of Akkaraipattu as an adolescent to pursue his secondary education at Zahira College in Colombo. After marrying Jezima's mother Farlina, he proceeded to qualify as an engineer. Sahid Ahamed was conversant in four languages – English, Tamil, Sinhalese, and Arabic – and had an excellent knowledge of the Koran. Though Jezima and her two sisters learned to recite the Koran from the Imam, he was adamant that they only learned the *meaning* of the Koran from him. Jezima's mother, who hailed from an upper-class background and was educated by governesses, enormously admired her husband and learned much from him about the interpretation of the Koran. Jezima too, through her father, came to understand God as loving and merciful, not as one who simply judged and punished from above. To this day, she remains thankful for the omnipresent and intimate role that God plays in her life; she hands over her difficulties to him yet also accepts whatever he hands down to her.

The Ahamed family was always a loving and tightly-knit household. Jezima charmingly observes that, to this day, "all three sisters adore each other." When her elder sister Zahira was tragically left a widow in the care of her young child at the age of 26, their father insisted that they return to their family home, which he had made large enough for everyone to live together under one roof. Zahira has been a second mother to Jezima's own three children and indeed, the children of all three sisters are exceedingly close, regarding each other as siblings rather than cousins. Jezima regards it as a wonderful blessing that members of all generations in her family enjoy the blessing of open communication, so that they always feel free to say anything to each other.

Jezima received her primary and secondary education at the prestigious St Bridget's Convent in Colombo, an environment which provided some valuable life lessons. As her own family was comfortable but not rich, Jezima remembers being struck by her friends' fabulous birthday parties. She dearly wanted a grand party of her own but her father simply refused to cooperate. One year, the young Jezima went ahead and invited her classmates anyway, hoping for a paternal change of heart, but to her disappointment, her father stood his ground. She was forced to buy her own birthday cake at the last minute from the local *kade* – a veritable fiasco! Her father came to her that night and said: "That's a good lesson for you. We are not the elite and I wouldn't like you to lead that kind of lifestyle." Years later, however, he hosted a beautiful party for her fifteenth birthday, after wisely explaining to Jezima that she was now mature enough to understand that although this was not their usual lifestyle, they occasionally needed to return the hospitality of other people.

At St Bridget's, Jezima excelled in her schoolwork, consistently winning prizes for coming first in class. After completing her final school examinations, she proceeded to the beautiful Peradeniya campus of the University of Ceylon, from which she graduated with a Bachelor of Arts in 1955. She recalls being the first girl from her ancestral village – Sainthamaruthu in the country's Eastern Province – to enter university, where she dreamed of gaining an English honours degree and partaking in her favourite extra-curricular activities of singing, dance and drama.

Unfortunately, however, repressive social practices turned her campus experience into a less idyllic and fulfilling one. While at Peradeniya, she was harassed by several boys from her community, who did not allow her to mix socially with Sinhalese boys and pestered her with letters and marriage proposals. One of these youths even threatened to kidnap her. Jezima's father, knowing what his daughter was enduring, asked Jezima to return to Colombo and study law there instead. Since she did not want to switch courses, he asked her to finish her studies at Peradeniya as quickly as possible, even if it meant putting her English studies on hold and graduating with a general arts degree instead.

No sooner had she returned home, Jezima's father steered her into a teaching job. Thus began Jezima's long and illustrious career as an educator. She started teaching at Devi Balika, which had been founded just a few years earlier, in 1953. The initial experience of teaching there came as a bit of a shock to the young graduate, who found it vastly different to her own schooling environment at St Bridget's. She remembers the Devi Balika building as being quite run-down, teeming with snakes on one side and kabaragoyas on the other! She soon realised, however, that it was the people, not the building, that mattered and in that respect, Devi Balika was a wonderful school. It was blessed with dedicated students and staff, and an excellent Principal – Mrs Wimala de Silva – who was a mentor to Jezima until she died in 2007.

Though she began working at Devi Balika at her father's behest and did not enjoy it much initially, Jezima later came to love teaching. In hindsight, it was the best career choice for her, as it allowed her the privilege of educating the younger generation as well as doing many other things. From the outset, Jezima was not a conventional teacher. Devi Balika provided her with a very flexible and personalised timetable, so that she could essentially schedule her own hours. This allowed her to engage in a number of different activities beyond teaching English in the classroom, such as drama and singing (particularly operettas), while also working on curriculum development. Jezima added to her busy schedule by singing and broadcasting on Radio Ceylon, where she presented programs in English of general interest as well as on Islamic subjects.

Nobody complained about Jezima's extensive range of outside involvements, partly because Devi Balika was a new school which within a few years had built an excellent reputation in both academic and non-academic spheres, including in co-curricular activities like singing. Jezima recalls that her father, using his skills as an engineer, built an open-air stage for drama and musical activities at the school. Sahid Ahamed remained a guiding force in her life and work until he died in 1972. Jezima's dear mother Farlina lived for another decade, passing away in 1983.

Jezima taught at Devi Balika over the course of nineteen years, during which her life witnessed a sea of events and changes, both professionally and personally. At a professional level, she twice left Devi Balika temporarily to complete further studies abroad; first to Canada, where she graduated with a Master of Arts (Education) from the renowned McGill University in 1966, and second to Australia, where she obtained a Diploma in TEFL (Teaching English as a Foreign Language) from the University of Sydney in 1972. In 1978, she began studying for her PhD but due to other commitments, never completed it. While she has some regrets about this, she rightly observes that the wealth of knowledge and experience she gained elsewhere might have advanced her beyond a doctorate.

At a personal level, it was during her tenure at Devi Balika that Jezima became a wife and mother. She had been a mere five years old when she first met her future husband – Mahroof Ismail – who was then only nine years of age. Of course, it was not until much later that they became romantically interested in each other; Jezima recalls that Mahroof suddenly became quite keen on her after her fourteenth birthday, perhaps because she had become a little better looking by this age! Although it was a so-called 'love-match', both sets of parents had secretly wanted their children to be together. Hence the two families warmly received the marriage between Jezima and Mahroof in 1958, just as they had welcomed the marriage between Jezima's older sister and Mahroof's brother in the previous year. Mahroof Ismail qualified as a doctor in 1957 and would later become Director of the Medical Research Institute, Professor of Parasitology, Dean of the Faculty of Medicine, and finally, Emeritus Professor, at the University of Colombo.

The Ismails were blessed with three children, two sons and then a daughter, who were born in 1960, 1962 and 1968 respectively. Jezima took maternity leave after all three births but even after she returned to work, she always used to return home by the early afternoon. It became apparent that her teaching career was an advantage rather than disadvantage to her children, for it afforded her the skills and time to teach them in a range of subjects, including Islam, English, Literature, Social Studies, Government and History, as well as to nurture their extra-curricular interests and activities. The Ismails' elder son is now a banker, the second is a director of a pharmaceutical company, while their youngest child is a speech pathologist. Jezima notes with pleasure that all of them also speak, sing and act well. She clearly relishes her time and efforts in raising her children, sagaciously remarking: "When you have children, they don't belong to you – you belong to them."

Jezima also taught her sisters' children and now delights in teaching her grand-daughters and great-nephews and nieces, who refuse to be taught English by anyone else! Regardless of whom she taught – whether her children, other younger members of her family, or her students at school – Jezima found that she loved teaching. It was enormously satisfying to have her students, some of whom were not good in English, suddenly see the light and meaning in a poem. In most of the O-level classes she taught, there were about 35 students; a couple of them would gain credit passes and all the rest would be awarded distinctions. Jezima attributes their excellent results not so much to the amount they studied but rather, to the genuine love they developed for English language and literature – so much so, that many swiftly learned poems by heart.

Like the happy family life of her girlhood, Jezima's family life after marriage has been filled with mutual love and respect. Jezima is fortunate to have a husband whom she considers a true friend and a model of equanimity – describing him as "very impartial and devoid of ego" – as well as a mother-in-law who brims with unconditional love for others. Jezima readily acknowledges that it was the unbridled support of her sisters, parents, husband, children and parents-in-law which made it easy for her to do all the things she wanted. Her elder sister Zahira took responsibility for the children's meals and clothes, feeding them with careful attention to their nutrition and diets. Meanwhile, her other sister Latheefa – a painter and art teacher – or her father would ferry the children (and Jezima) to and from school. All three sisters tutored the children in various subjects, with English naturally being Jezima's domain. It was thus a combined effort to raise their daughters and sons, within an extended family system borne not of compulsion but of choice. Together, the entire family is bound by a shared set of values and in particular, they all resolutely believe in education and learning as a critical foundation in life.

Jezima eventually left Devi Balika in 1975 to become Principal at Muslim Ladies' College (MLC), a position which she held for thirteen years. She found the school to be a very different one to Devi Balika and hence it was not an easy transition. Her progressive ideas and intended reforms, especially those aimed at enabling the students to compete equally with girls in non-Muslim schools, did not sit well with some Muslim leaders who reacted by mounting public attacks on Jezima's work and character. She often wondered if she could continue in her job but thanks to the support of her family, the parent body at MLC, and like-minded members of the community, she continued in her responsibilities. In the midst of these trying times, she was especially buoyed by the strength of her husband, who emphasised the importance

Receiving the award of Deshabandu from President Premadasa, 1986

As principal of Muslim Ladies' College

of not running away from a challenge and assured her that together, they would face all difficulties as a team.

While serving as Principal of MLC, Jezima continued to extend her involvement and leadership in other areas. In 1980, she became the first woman appointed to the Board of Directors of the Sri Lanka Broadcasting Corporation (SLBC) and served as Acting Chairperson of SLBC. Jezima also contributed to the establishment and operation of several NGOs which continue to be important social forces in Sri Lanka today, especially for the advancement of women in the country. An important example of her pioneering social advocacy is the critical role she played in founding the Muslim Women's Research and Action Forum (MWRAF) in 1976, which is well-known for its work in empowering Muslim women, especially in Sri Lanka but also abroad. The next year, she founded the Academy of Adult Education for Women (AAEW), an organisation which she still chairs. From 1982 to 1983, Jezima presided over the Sri Lanka Federation of University Women (SLFUW). In addition, she worked to establish the Sri Lanka Muslim Women's Conference (SLMWC), an umbrella organisation for several Muslim women's groups. She continues to serve as President of the SLMWC to this day.

After prematurely retiring as Principal of

MLC in 1988, Jezima expanded, rather than reduced, her work in various fields. During the 1990s, she travelled overseas on several occasions as a member of international election monitoring committees. She was a member of the South Asian Association for Regional Cooperation (SAARC) monitoring committees on the National Elections in Pakistan and Bangladesh in 1993 and 1996, respectively, and of the Commonwealth Observer Mission to oversee the Presidential Election in Nigeria in 1999. In the course of this decade, Jezima also founded and was President of two notable organisations which promote educational access and equity; the Sri Lanka Association for the Advancement of Education (SLAAED), and the SAARC Federation of University Women. In 2000, she was appointed to the National Committee on Women, a group which works under the Minister of Child Development and Women's Empowerment to help women in Sri Lanka enjoy fundamental freedoms and human rights on an equal basis with men. Her work in human rights also encompasses serving on the Board of Management of the Centre for the Study of Human Rights (CSHR), an institution attached to the Faculty of Law at the University of Colombo which furthers the awareness and implementation of human rights in Sri Lanka. Indeed, Jezima is widely respected and consulted by human rights organisations both within and outside Sri Lanka for her wisdom and expertise on a range of issues, especially those pertaining to education, women, and the Muslim community.

In recent years, Jezima has extended her influence in education and the non-governmental sector. Most significantly, she was inaugurated in 2003 as the Chancellor of South Eastern University of Sri Lanka, thereby becoming the first Muslim woman to hold such a position (and the second Sri Lankan woman to do so, following in the footsteps of the founding principal of Devi Balika, Mrs Wimala de Silva, who was Chancellor of Sri Jayawardenepura University for many years). Meanwhile, she has continued to dedicate her time and energy to numerous NGOs. Thus, for example, she is a governor of both the Marga Institute – an organisation devoted to evaluating development practices in Sri Lanka – as well as of the Alcohol and Drug Information Centre (ADIC). Latterly, she has been actively involved with HelpAge in Sri Lanka as a member of its council; aptly reflecting her stated view that by middle-age, one should prepare for growing old, so that it will not come as an unwelcome surprise!

That Jezima is held in high esteem by a cross-section of governmental and non-governmental communities in Sri Lanka is amply demonstrated by her appointment to so many influential organisations, commissions and committees; frequently as their only female member. She has also received recognition in the form of several national and international awards. Hence she has won awards from the internationally-affiliated Zonta and Lions Clubs for her work in education, and is an Ambassador for Peace of the Interreligious and International Federation for World Peace (IIFWP). Most notably, she was conferred in 1989 the title of Deshabandu, one of the highest-ranking civilian honours that a Sri Lankan citizen can receive. When asked what she considers her most significant achievement, Jezima fittingly responds that it is "to be loved by the many around me as a human being."

Even after attaining prominence for her work and activism, however, Jezima continued to face censure in certain quarters. When Yusuf Islam – formerly known as Cat Stevens – visited Sri Lanka and wanted to meet with her, conservative leaders urged him not to, disapprovingly pointing to Jezima being the only woman on commissions and sometimes having to travel with men. Yusuf Islam proceeded to meet her anyway, and later opined that of the many Muslim activists he had met around the world, he considered her one of the best. To Jezima's credit, she has always endured her critics with grace, dignity and fortitude. When she received the award of Deshabandu, for example, many were speculating as to how she would react when President Ranasinghe Premadasa garlanded her. At the apposite moment during the ceremony, she simply took the garland out of his hands and put it around her neck, thereby averting any criticism of being garlanded by a man. Jezima notes that she never rebelled against authority, yet equally, did not shy from marking her presence.

It is a testament to Jezima's boundless energy and range of expertise that it is simply impossible to describe each of her countless civic roles and achievements. It must suffice to say that she has made an extraordinarily wide-ranging contribution to the socio-economic development of Sri Lanka, most notably with regard to women (especially Muslim women), education, community services, and human rights. In looking back at her life, Jezima observes that every few years, she has taken on something totally different in her life – whether pursuing an educational qualification, accepting a new job, establishing a different social organisation, or foraying into a new area such as broadcasting, election monitoring, or university leadership – but that each of these paths has been tremendously fulfilling.

The devastation wrought by the tsunami in 2004 marked another defining moment in Jezima's thinking and activism. After that catastrophic event and her experiences in rebuilding and rehabilitation in the eastern parts of the country, she has become more convinced of the need to challenge the whole system in Sri Lanka in order to create a holistic mechanism that works towards democracy, non-discrimination, and greater equity and justice. Believing that there needs to be an alternative to everyday politics in bringing about this mechanism of change, she has turned her thoughts to how to inspire transformative social leadership, so as to empower women and men of all communities in Sri Lanka. We might all feel fortunate that Jezima Ismail views the mission of social leadership – of which Sri Lanka has been largely bereft in recent times – as integral to her spiritual and personal journey in life. She is a lady uniquely positioned to fulfil this important mission, given her far-reaching experience of the nation's educational, social and developmental issues, and moreover, her enduring wisdom and dynamism in tackling them.

With her husband Professor Mahroof Ismail, 1985

K.G. Badra Gunawardena at the Asian Games, Bangkok, 1970

K.G. Badra Gunawardena
Sportswoman

To hold three national sprinting records, in the 100, 200 and 400-metre events, as well as the 100 and 200-metre national records for as long as twenty years, are extraordinary feats. These are the achievements of Kahande Gamage Badra – better known as "K.G. Badra" – who in attaining these milestones etched her name into Sri Lanka's sporting annals for generations to come. Having virtually dominated women's track in the country for more than a decade, it is small wonder that she remains among the nation's most recognised names in athletics.

K.G. Badra was only eighteen years old when, in 1968, the general public acknowledged her as a bright young star by voting her Most Popular Sportswoman of the Year in an annual competition sponsored by the *Times of Ceylon*. She garnered the same accolade the following year, together with another prestigious award, Sportswoman of the Year. Besides excelling on the track, Badra has committed herself to the development and administration of Sri Lankan athletics for over thirty years through her employment at the Ministry of Sports, where she now holds the senior position of Assistant Director, Department of Sports Development.

Badra hails from the town of Galle on the country's southern coast. Her father, K.G. Francis Appuhamy, was a successful businessman there and her mother, Ciciliana Munasinghe, was a capable housewife who shouldered the task of rearing three sons and two daughters. Born the youngest in her family on 17th January 1950, Badra received her primary education at Sangamitta Vidyalaya, Galle. Badra holds fond memories of her childhood centred around their family home, which was situated on a hilltop in the Madawalamulla area, a few kilometres outside the town centre.

Badra recalls having great fun with her cousins, who were around her age and lived in a house at the base of the hill. Whenever she had time to play, she would run down the hill to her cousins' home, returning home via the alternate route of a hundred or so steps alongside the road. It so happened that the primary school she attended was also on a hill, and just as she did during playtime at home, she would joyfully run up and down the hill on her way to and from school. It was in this carefree manner that Badra unknowingly entered into athletic training at an early age. From this simple beginning, it

Badra meeting Queen Elizabeth II at the Commonwealth Games, Edinburgh, 1970

seemed almost a natural progression for her to enter the running events at her primary school sports meets. She ran enthusiastically each year, winning enough certificates and trophies as "Miss K.G. Badra" to draw the attention of many spectators.

Badra was, however, exposed to life's inevitable tragedies when as a nine-year-old girl, she lost her twelve-year-old brother, to whom she was very close. In 1960, not long after this traumatic time for her family, her parents sent Badra and her other siblings to Colombo for their education. They chose Buddhist Ladies' College (BLC) for their two daughters, ten year old Badra and her older sister Sumana who was eight years senior. Badra feels fortunate that she was not alone at boarding school, for Sumana was a like a surrogate mother to her – she was always there to turn to and made it easier for Badra to adjust to hostel life. Indeed, observes Badra, "even now, she still mothers me"!

None of Badra's family members was known to have had notable sporting inclinations. Even so, Badra always seemed naturally sports-minded and at BLC, she took an active interest in netball and athletics. It was in the latter that Badra excelled. While representing her house in the sports meet during her first year at school, she won every event in which she participated. The then sports teacher at BLC, Mrs Mallika de Silva, quickly spotted Badra's prodigious talent and took a keen interest in furthering her athletic development. Due to the lack of on-site sporting facilities at BLC, however, students needed to be taken to the nearby Victoria Park (now the Viharamahadevi Park) to train. Badra looked forward to those sessions not only because she enjoyed the training, but also because it provided her a welcome escape from the confines of the hostel! Although a mischievous schoolgirl, she recalls that she was also a popular student who showed natural leadership qualities, becoming a school prefect, the Games Captain and Netball Captain.

In 1966, Badra qualified for the All Island Schools Athletics Championships to compete in the Under-16 sprints in the 100 and 200 metres. Accompanied by Mrs de Silva, she enthusiastically made the journey to the competition venue in Anuradhapura to prove herself at the inter-school level, and proceeded to win the 200-metre event. Her success marked a moment of realisation for Badra, when she felt she 'discovered herself' and her ability to run.

After completing the GCE O-level examination in the sciences, Badra entered Holy Family Convent (HFC) Bambalapitiya in 1968 where she believed there were better sporting facilities and a stronger athletics team than at BLC. Miss Trixie Jayasuriya, then the Games

Mistress and a part-time netball coach at HFC, was instrumental in her move – most likely because she recognised young Badra's athletic potential. By this time, Badra was enjoying running and winning so much that she switched to studying Home Sciences at HFC, in the hope of freeing up more time for sports. Badra was fortunate that her family allowed her to make her own choices, rather than pressuring her to choose academics over sports, or vice versa.

Whilst at HFC, Badra rapidly gained a reputation as a new star of the track, with impressive performances in sprints at inter-school meets and open championships, enabling her to collect "Best Performance" trophies on numerous occasions. One of the highlights during her HFC days was the 1968 All Island Inter School Athletics Championships where she won the 100 and 200 metres sprint double and the Under-19 4x100 metre relay as a member of the HFC team. Not only was Badra triumphant on the track that year, but the HFC netball team of which she was a member – playing the position of wing defence – also won the All Island (Senior) Netball Trophy.

It was thus hardly surprising that Badra was amongst the chosen few included in the national athletics squad in 1968. Naturally, she was overjoyed at gaining entry onto the national stage. It was an important milestone for the schoolgirl, opening the door for her to represent Sri Lanka internationally – a challenge that she eagerly awaited.

That international opportunity presented itself soon enough, when Badra was selected to compete in the 1968 Thailand National Championships in Bangkok. She had to overcome some initial obstacles, including the decision of the Amateur Athletics Association (AAA) not to fund her, on the grounds that she was still in school. Perturbed by the prospect of Badra's non-inclusion in the team, the then Minister for Education – Dr W. Dahanayake, who also hailed from Galle – spoke to her father about the possibility of funding her. Not wanting his daughter to miss a great opportunity, he decided to pay for Badra's passage to Bangkok, paving the way for her to proceed to Thailand.

Even with minimal training at the national level, Badra earned gold medals in both the 100 and 200-metre events, and lowered the Thai national 100-metres record with a timing of 12.4 seconds. It was her best timing yet and even she was amazed at what she accomplished. Considering that she was still a schoolgirl and it was her first overseas appearance, it was indeed an impressive accomplishment. Upon her victorious return home as the only athlete in the Sri Lanka team to win "double gold", Badra was warmly received at the airport by Dr

Dahanayake himself, joined by Badra's parents, HFC teachers, students and other well-wishers.

Not long after she was crowned 'Most Popular Sportswoman of the Year' and 'Sportswoman of the Year' in 1969 at Colombo's Sugathadasa Indoor Stadium amidst a huge gathering of spectators, Badra's alma mater Sangamitta Vidyalaya invited her as a VIP guest to the school sports meet – a meet in which she herself had competed not so long ago as a primary school student. As it happened, Dr Dahanayake was also invited as a VIP guest to that meet. Once again, he was instrumental in facilitating an opportunity for Badra's progress; this time, by speaking to the Director of the Ministry of Sports, Dr H.S.R. Goonewardene – who was present as the Chief Guest – and persuading him to consider Badra for training overseas.

This led to a tremendous opportunity for Badra, an offer of a sports scholarship to Germany, fully funded by the German government – testimony to the now national recognition of Badra's talent and prowess. It seems that this offer sealed her fate; Badra decided to pursue amateur athletics on a full-time basis, a major step forward and a decision she made with great support from her family. One of her older brothers, K.G. Karunasena, was Badra's constant mentor and guide, ardently encouraging her throughout her career even though he himself was not a sportsman.

At the 1969 Ceylon Track and Field Club (CT & FC) Open Championships, prior to her departure for Germany, Badra stamped her name into Sri Lankan sporting history by shattering the 100- metre national record previously held by Lorraine Rutnam with a timing of 12.2 seconds. In 1970, she did it again, this time in the 200 metres when she bettered Priyanthi Gunasekara's record with a timing of 25.7 seconds.

She left for Germany in 1970 to commence a rigorous three-month training course at the Sport University in Cologne (now the German Sport University Cologne.) The facilities in Cologne were superb and presented a rare opportunity for Badra's progress. Moreover, it was a revealing and maturing experience for young Badra. The territory was unfamiliar and she felt lonely and nervous, especially having to deal with language and cultural differences. She candidly discloses how taken aback she was when asked to go on dates, a practice alien to her own upbringing. She is thankful to a South African lady instructor who became her confidante and guided and advised her throughout her stay.

While in Germany, Badra continued to improve, and bettered her own Sri Lankan 100-metre record, clocking 11.9 seconds at the 1970 Cologne City meet and becoming the first

Badra in her office at the Sports Ministry

Badra at Johannes Gutenberg Universität, Mainz, Germany, 1986

Sri Lankan woman to break the 12-second mark. It was a personal best, and it impressed the Sri Lankan authorities. She was selected to compete in the 100-metre event at the Commonwealth Games in Edinburgh, Scotland that same year, thus gaining the distinction of becoming Sri Lanka's first female representative at any Commonwealth Games. Badra was Sri Lanka's sole representative and so was bestowed with the additional honour of carrying the national flag – a proud and momentous experience for her.

Badra remembers the extravaganza of the post-Games Garden Party hosted by Queen Elizabeth II at a palace in Edinburgh, to which only one representative from each competing country was invited. It appears that the organisers ensured that the invitees were well cared for, even arranging for a team of make-up artists and hairdressers to groom them for this grand occasion! Badra attired herself in a maroon and gold saree which she recalls as being her maiden appearance in saree. To meet the Queen was indeed a rare privilege for the young Badra. "Although I did not win a medal, it was a wonderful experience," she recalls of her journey to the United Kingdom.

A few months after the Commonwealth Games, Badra competed at the 1970 Asian Games held in Bangkok, where she placed fifth in the 100 metres. 1971 was yet another defining year for Badra. She was one of a select few athletes from Asian countries who were picked to train in Munich, Germany, in preparation for the 1972 Olympic Games there. To her delight, the pool included three athletes from Sri Lanka, the other two being sprinter Sunil Gunawardena – who would later become Badra's husband – and S.L.B. Rosa, the long distance runner who became known as the "barefoot" marathoner some years later, and who had won the Most Popular Sportsman of the Year award in 1968, the same year that Badra won in the female category.

In Germany for a second time, she was persuaded by her coach to train seriously for the 400 metres. Badra rose admirably to this new challenge; at some training meets, she defeated even the Asian Games gold medalist, Kamaljit Sandhu, in this event. After returning to Sri Lanka, she went on to lower the 400-metre national record in 1972 that had been held by Indrani Jayaweera. Badra could hardly await the dawn of the Olympics in Munich, but fate dealt her a cruel blow. A few weeks prior to the opening of the Games in August 1972, she was diagnosed with hepatitis, which shattered her dreams of travelling to Munich and becoming an Olympian.

Soon after her recovery from hepatitis, Badra decided to commence paid employment.

As her training was scheduled in the evenings, she had an open calendar during the day. Badra joined the Ceylon Transport Board (CTB) as a clerk in 1972. One reason she joined the CTB was that Sunil Gunawardena, whom she had met the previous year and who was by then a close friend, was already employed by the CTB. Within three months, however, Badra left the CTB to join the Ministry of Sports as a Sports Officer. There she was charged with training athletes and other sportspersons – a role more in line with her interests.

Even while working at the Ministry, Badra continued her own running and training. Among the highlights of this period was her participation at the 1974 Asian Games in Tehran, where she qualified for the finals in the 400 metres. By the time Badra retired from competitive running in 1977, she had bagged a haul of nine gold medals for Sri Lanka in the 100, 200, and 400-metre events, in places as far-flung as India, Singapore, Thailand, Iran, Germany and Scotland.

In the meantime, Badra and Sunil's relationship had continued to develop to the point that they became romantically linked. Their plans to get married, however, were delayed due to opposition from both sets of parents on the grounds of religious differences– she is a Buddhist and he, a Catholic. Fortunately, a happy ending prevailed upon this impasse. After seven years of courtship, love eventually triumphed, and they wed in 1978 with the blessings of their parents.

Sunil too was a star runner in Sri Lankan sprinting, and is an Olympian and Asian Games gold medalist. As high-achieving sportspersons, Badra and Sunil had a mutual respect and understanding of each other's aspirations and were aware of the challenges of competitive sport. This meant that they were able to complement and encourage each other in the pursuit of their individual goals.

Badra attributes her success to several factors. She cites her childhood environment in Galle, where she would routinely run up and down the hills, as enabling her to strengthen her legs at an early age and providing her with the initial impetus. At school, she received inspiring guidance from the BLC and HFC sports mistresses, whilst her time in Germany provided well structured training at a more formal and international level. She received tremendous support from her husband Sunil, and worked closely with several local coaches, including Mr K.L.F. Wijedasa from the University of Colombo and Mr Lakshman de Alwis from the Ministry of Sports. Badra believes her success in athletics required not only physical prowess but also mental strength. Although formal psychological training was not available during her days, her confidence was boosted by attending leading Colombo schools and gaining exposure to national and international events.

At the Ministry of Sports, Badra seized an opportunity to enter sports coaching. She was made an athletics coach in 1980, becoming one of four persons holding this position and the first woman to do so. To be eligible for this promotion, she had to complete a nine-month Diploma in Sports which was conducted by the Ministry. The transition into coaching was a natural step for Badra and she slipped into it with ease. Her capabilities ensured she was later selected for an eighteen-month programme in athletics coaching at the Johannes Gutenberg-Universität Mainz in Germany, again with the sponsorship of the German government. It was Badra's third trip to Germany and allowed her to acquire fluency in German, having been compelled to study the language for six months as a pre-requisite to the course.

Badra graduated from the programme in Mainz in 1986 with a Diploma and a First Class in Sprints. She views this result in the context of excelling in a challenging assignment where she was required to motivate a group of more than twelve children and perfect their sprint "start" technique. She could not have hoped for a better assignment, for, being a sprinter herself, she found this project particularly suited to her strengths and experience.

Unlike the many athletes of her era who left the country, Badra has for over thirty years patriotically dedicated her services to the Ministry and to the development of athletics in Sri Lanka in her positions as Sports Officer, Athletics Coach, Project Officer in athletics and since 1995, Assistant Director, Department of Sports Development. She has trained aspiring athletes at many of Colombo's leading schools, steering hopeful stars towards success. Among her trainees are several of Sri Lanka's national record holders in track and field events, including in the 100 metres, long jump and hurdles events. Having endured the constraints in local resources during her own athletic career, Badra aspired to improve the level of coaching and training equipment throughout the country. Her current position charges her with maintaining the training grounds at Independence Square, as well as at twenty or so district training centres, to which she makes regular visits, spotting talent and conducting selection camps.

In addition, she contributes her time to a number of athletics associations, and has held several honorary positions, including Vice President of the Sri Lanka Athletics Association. As a council member of the Women's Asian Amateur Athletics Federation (from 1996 to 1999), she had the privilege of attending a 1997 committee meeting held in Jakarta, Indonesia. Badra also travelled to Namibia to represent

Sri Lanka at the 1998 World Conference on Women and Sport. "There was no money in the sport in my days. Coaching was minimal and one relied heavily on talent. Now of course, it is a profession," observes Badra. Her inherent love for athletics and constant flow of achievements (she has amassed plenty of silver and has a cupboard dedicated to holding her precious trophies) helped sustain her desire to win.

Badra encourages girls to take up competitive athletics. "They can earn from it now. Training outdoors with other athletes is a form of relaxation and beneficial health-wise. It is also possible to combine sports with the role of a good housewife," she says. She considers herself as an example of how one can embark on a rewarding journey in athletics from amateur athlete, to athletics coach, to administrator – adding that there are far greater opportunities and avenues open nowadays to pursue a passion in sports. Her advice to aspiring young athletes reflects the wisdom of her professional and personal experience. She counsels them to "be modest about one's achievements and help one another," noting that this holistic approach "will foster a sense of satisfaction and happiness."

Kumari Jayawardena at a Trade Union meeting, 1962

Kumari Jayawardena
Social Scientist & Activist

Kumari Jayawardena defies an easy description. Her work and passions span many fields that are diverse yet coherent – from academia and the social sciences (especially political science), to socialism and workers' rights, to feminist theory and advocacy. Kumari's life has blended both reflection and action on important social issues.

How did this thinker and activist come into her own? For a start, her parentage and upbringing were rather unusual, especially in the era of her birth. She was born in London in 1931 to a Sri Lankan father from Randombe (a village between Balapitiya and Ambalangoda, on the southern coast of Sri Lanka) and a British mother from Durham, England. Her mother, Eleanor Hutton, from a socialist, agnostic family, was drawn to Buddhism as a young woman and had met Kumari's father, Dr A. P. de Zoysa, at the Buddhist Mission in London while he was studying in the city. They married in London in 1929 and returned to Sri Lanka five years later. Kumari was their only child.

As a young girl, Kumari's immediate family provided her earliest models of leading a life in the public sphere. Eleanor de Zoysa taught music at Ananda Balika Vidyalaya, a Buddhist girls' school in Colombo, and was active in the women's movement in Sri Lanka. Dr A.P. de Zoysa entered political life upon his return to Sri Lanka and served as a member for Colombo South in the State Council from 1936 to 1947. In Kumari's words, he was a "maverick politician" who espoused causes that were unpopular at the time, including the abolition of dowries and the entry of women into the public services.

He exemplified to Kumari the importance of pursuing and championing a cause that she truly believed in, irrespective of what others may think. Aside from her parents, Kumari's maternal grandfather, a socialist, was in the British trade union movement and her grandmother was involved in the suffragette movement in Britain. Her mother's four sisters were also role models by pursuing careers of their own – three of them also being politically active on the Left.

Outside her family circle, Kumari was greatly influenced by Dr S.A. Wickremasinghe and his wife Doreen, who were both leading figures of the Left. Dr S.A. Wickremasinghe was a founder of the Lanka Sama Samaja Party (popularly known as the LSSP) and subsequently of the Communist Party, whilst the British-born Doreen Wickremasinghe (née Young) led the anti-imperialist *Suriya Mal* movement and was later elected to Parliament as a member of the Communist Party. They were both friends of Kumari's parents, and Doreen was also principal of Ananda Balika Vidyalaya while Kumari's mother taught music there. Doreen affectionately called Kumari's mother 'Schubert'. The closeness of the families was such that Kumari spent considerable time with the Wickremasinghes (and with their children, Suriya and Suren), affording her an intimate insight into progressive causes at an early age.

Kumari was thus raised in an atypical milieu. She was surrounded by people who lived and worked in the public domain, in pursuit of important social causes. The options of working in the private sector, or not having a career at all, simply did not present themselves to her. It seemed entirely normal to pursue a career in the public domain and to weave politics – especially socialist politics – into one's everyday life and work.

In addition to the role models within her family environment, other factors helped instill in Kumari a sense of independence and inner strength. Growing up, she lived in Colombo and was educated at Ladies' College, a school which in her view fostered the development of independent young women. Periodically, she would make short visits to London to see her maternal relations. These sojourns made her realise that she was perceived as 'different' in England, as well as in Sri Lanka, since she was Eurasian and seen as neither entirely English nor wholly Sri Lankan. Although Kumari was sensitive about her unusual heritage during her schooldays, often wishing she were a 'typical' Sinhalese, she later saw being exposed to two cultures as an advantage.

After completing her secondary education, Kumari left Sri Lanka in 1952 to enter the prestigious London School of Economics (LSE). Graduating from the LSE with a BSc (Econ) in 1955, she proceeded to Paris, where she obtained the *Certificat d'Etudes Politiques* from the Institut des Sciences Politiques in 1956. She then headed back to London, where she qualified as a barrister from Lincoln's Inn in 1958 and in 1964, received a PhD in industrial relations from the LSE. With these impressive academic credentials, Kumari returned to Sri Lanka in 1964. In 1958, she married Lal Jayawardena, a Cambridge-educated economist whom she had met in England. Lal shared many of Kumari's intellectual interests and, until he passed away in 2004, fully supported her scholarship and activism. The couple had their only child, Rohan, in 1964.

In 1969, Kumari Jayawardena embarked on

her academic career, when she began teaching political science at the Vidyodaya University (now the University of Sri Jayewardenepura) and the University of Colombo. Her tenure at the University of Colombo eventually spanned sixteen years, during which Kumari became an internationally acclaimed scholar and came to play a leading role in social and political movements in Sri Lanka. From 1980 to 1982, she had the opportunity of teaching abroad, at the Institute of Social Studies in The Hague, Netherlands. In 1987-88, she spent a year in the United States as an Affiliated Fellow of the Bunting Institute at Radcliffe College, the renowned women's college which has since become part of Harvard University. Although Kumari retired from her post of Associate Professor in 1985, she continued to teach at the University of Colombo on its Master's Programme in Women's Studies.

Around the time she began lecturing, Kumari became increasingly active in social and political movements. In 1971, the year that Sri Lanka was rocked by an insurrection, she was a founding member of the Civil Rights Movement, which continues to this day to advocate human rights for all Sri Lankans. Following the ethnic riots of 1977, she was instrumental with other academics in establishing the Social Scientists Association (SSA), an organisation devoted to fighting communalism and chauvinism of all kinds in Sri Lanka and to research and publication. The SSA originated in a small group of social scientists who began meeting to discuss the causes of the 1977 riots. The group continued their meetings and eventually decided to formalise them by establishing the SSA. Kumari still plays a leading role in the SSA, and continues to work from her office on their premises in Colombo. She explains that the movement's "initial task was to demythologise history". It was in furtherance of this mission that Kumari wrote one of her most controversial books, *Ethnic and Class Conflicts in Sri Lanka: Some Aspects of Sinhala-Buddhist Consciousness over the Last One Hundred Years* (1996). Although the SSA focuses on local history and politics, Kumari notes that it has also drawn inspiration from similar movements worldwide, including in India and Tanzania.

Kumari gradually became deeply involved in both the labour movement and the women's movement. The intellectual foundations of her work in the labour movement were laid in London, when she wrote her doctoral thesis on the history of the trade union movement. Upon her return to Sri Lanka, Kumari began attending trade union meetings and in 1972, Duke University Press published her book entitled *The Rise of the Labor Movement in Ceylon* based on her PhD thesis. In 1977, she and other university teachers established a workers'

education programme for trade unionists and other workers, which was taught by a staff that included several eminent academics.

When asked whether her relative affluence hindered her work as a socialist and in the labour movement, Kumari frankly acknowledges that there were people who considered her 'bourgeois'. She firmly believes, however, in being judged by the work you do. As she explains, one's social background does not prevent an understanding of fundamental problems in society and a desire for social change. She laments the frequent misconception that to be a socialist, one must somehow live in a working-class milieu. Kumari notes that many people see the intersection of her work and background in a more positive light, as becomes evident when they inadvertently preface praise of her work by comments such as "although she is from Colombo 7 …" and "although half-foreign …".

As a complement to her work in the labour movement, Kumari also travelled outside Sri Lanka to participate in international socialist meetings. It was during these meetings that she was first exposed to the international women's movement. Indeed, when pressed to state what she considers her "greatest achievement", Kumari cites her work in the women's movement, both locally and internationally. That work is, without question, pioneering, extensive and enduring.

Kumari has written and edited several books on feminism. Her first was a booklet entitled *Feminism is Relevant* which she wrote with two others in 1975 because so many at the time were decrying the relevance of feminism. The booklet was written in a 'question and answer' form, so as to be accessible to everyone from A-level students to academics. It was used abroad, including in India and Pakistan. She has since written several influential books, the most celebrated being *Feminism and Nationalism in the Third World* in 1986, which is now a standard text in women's studies programmes around the world. In 1992, it was selected by the iconic American feminist magazine, *Ms.*, as one of the 20 most important books of the feminist decades (1970-1990).

Kumari's work in the women's movement, however, extends well beyond her scholarship. In addition to teaching and writing on women's studies, she has spoken on behalf of women workers at trade union meetings, and worked to gender-sensitise school texts by urging the removal of sexist assumptions and language. In advance of the Sri Lankan parliamentary elections in 2000 and 2001, she played an active role in the meetings of twelve local women's groups, who together drafted a non-partisan "Women's Manifesto". The manifesto urged all parties contesting the elections to address a series of demands; these included quotas for women in

Parliament and local government, equal wages for both sexes, the repeal of discriminatory laws, and improved health care for women. In 2003, Kumari was appointed to the Sub-Committee on Gender Issues, which was formed by the Sri Lankan government and the Liberation Tigers of Tamil Eelam (LTTE) to integrate women's issues into the peace process. Her role in the Sub-Committee involved travelling to the country's north to meet with women members of the LTTE, where they discussed a wide range of issues, including personal security and safety, livelihood and employment, and resettlement. It was short-lived as the end of the peace talks meant that this Sub-Committee was dissolved.

Kumari also acts – formally and informally – as an advisor and mentor to countless individuals and groups working in the women's movement and other progressive causes. Hence, for example, she served on the board of CENWOR (Centre for Women's Research), a leading women's advocacy group in Sri Lanka. Radhika Coomaraswamy, the UN Secretary-General's Special Representative for Children and Armed Conflict, recently commented that Kumari Jayawardena nurtured so many scholars and activists in all parts of the world that she became known as the "mother of all mothers"!

Naturally, Kumari was herself inspired by other scholars and activists. When asked about her role models in Sri Lanka, beyond the considerable influence of her own family circle, she names Vivienne Goonewardena, the pioneering leftist and feminist, Anil de Silva, the author and art critic, and Doreen Wickremasinghe. Among those abroad, she has drawn inspiration from her friend, Romila Thapar, an Indian historian and anti-communalist whom Kumari came to know when they were both studying in London, as well as from the Indian activist Kamla Bhasin. Kumari's work in the women's movement has also been influenced by activists and intellectuals further afield. They include Sheila Rowbotham, the British socialist feminist who wrote the book *Hidden from History: 300 years of women's oppression and the fight against it*, and a global and regional network of women – especially South Asian women. Often, she would first become acquainted with these women through their writings and then would later actually meet them at conferences abroad. They still correspond and meet when possible, thereby maintaining a rich intellectual sorority.

Remarkably, Kumari Jayawardena shows no signs of slowing down her work, even though she retired from her university post over twenty years ago. If anything, she has become even more prolific in her 'retirement'. In the last two decades, she has written and edited several influential books, including *The White Woman's*

Lecturing at a women's workshop in Adyas, Chennai, November 1983

Other Burden: Western Women and South Asia During British Rule (1995), *Nobodies to Somebodies: The Rise of the Colonial Bourgeoisie in Sri Lanka* (2002), and *Erasure of the Euro-Asian: Recovering Early Radicalism & Feminism in South Asia* (2007), and most recently, *Perpetual Ferment: Popular revolts in Sri Lanka in the 18th and 19th centuries* (2010).

Many of Kumari's books have been translated into Sinhala and Tamil, enabling her to reach a wider audience. One of her newest works is *The Erasure of the Euro-Asian* (2007), which affirms the role played by Euro-Asians in South Asian history. Fittingly, a collection of essays entitled *At the Cutting Edge: Essays in Honour of Kumari Jayawardena* was published in 2007 in India by Women Unlimited. This tribute, which was edited by Neloufer de Mel and Selvy Thiruchandran, contains essays by prominent scholars and activists on the wide range of issues to which Kumari has devoted her life's work, including on gender, identity, culture, human rights, and the nation-state.

Given her pioneering role in the women's movement, it is especially opportune to hear Kumari's advice to younger women. When asked whether she would recommend a career in academia to those considering it, she replies that she thinks it is a good option for women. Academics have the opportunity to pursue interesting research

Kumari as a student in France, 1957

and to be in touch with the younger generation, which is exciting. Many female academics enjoy having more flexible hours than a standard '9 to 5' job and, like school teachers, they have longer periods of vacation.

However, an academic career is by no means the only path she would recommend to younger women. It is most important, advises Kumari, to be in the public domain rather than the private. This means not only working outside the home, but also working for the common good and not simply for private gain. Otherwise, as she explains, "When the children grow up, you will ask yourself 'what did I do with my life, where has it gone?' When you are doing something for someone else and you have a cause, your life is more satisfying even if you forego some money." There is no doubt that Kumari Jayawardena has lived true to her wise words. Her tireless advocacy for fundamental social change, both in Sri Lanka and abroad, has set an example for many to follow.

Kumari working on a manuscript, Colombo, late 1980s

Necklace by Mallika Hemachandra

Mallika Hemachandra
Jeweller

Mallika Hemachandra has been in the forefront of Sri Lanka's famed jewellery industry for over forty years. She received the prestigious 'Gold Award' in the Small Business Category at the Woman Entrepreneur of the Year Awards in 1997 from the Chamber of Industry and Commerce of Sri Lanka. More recently, in 2005, the then President Chandrika Bandaranaike Kumaratunga conferred on Mallika the national honour of Sri Lanka Sikhamani, in recognition of her outstanding contribution to the trade.

Over the past several decades, countless women have adorned themselves with her elegantly designed gold and gem-studded necklaces, bracelets, earrings, rings and other items of jewellery, which are all marketed through Mallika Hemachandra Jewellers (Pvt) Limited (MHJ). For children, she has crafted jewellery incorporating various Disney characters since she obtained the franchise in the early 1990's. Subsequently, Barbie Doll, Little Princess, Snow White and other popular fantasy characters were included in her collection. Exquisite cufflinks and tie-pins are featured amongst her glittering range of products, amply demonstrating that she has not forgotten the men folk!

Though Sri Lanka has long been renowned for its gems and jewellery, Mallika was not raised with a particular awareness and knowledge of the business. She was the eldest child of Dr W.M. Fernando, a busy medical practitioner, and his wife Kamala, a very efficient and talented lady who had a flair for making delicious cakes and desserts. Born on 6 June 1932, Mallika grew up at 73 Horton Place, Colombo where now stands the MHJ head office and main showroom.

She was fortunate to have experienced her schooldays under the leadership of Mrs Clara Motwani and Mrs Susan Pulimood, two legendary principals of Visakha Vidyalaya, where she studied throughout her primary and secondary education. "I was good in Science and was best at Zoology," she recalls, noting her success in entering the highly competitive science stream at Visakha, the prestigious and academically demanding girls' school where she was assured of a rigorous education. Throughout school, Mallika impressed her teachers with her drawings, in particular related to her Zoology dissections, frequently receiving the highest marks in class.

Mallika was a well-rounded student whose

Mallika with Queen Elizabeth II, Colombo, 1981

Mallika with Empress Michiko of Japan, Tokyo, 1985

interests extended beyond the academic sphere to music, arts and sports. A talented pianist, she passed a number of examinations conducted by Trinity College London, eventually obtaining the Licentiate (LTCL). Alongside, she learnt to play the violin, and as a schoolgirl recalls taking part in a memorable tour with a local philharmonic orchestra trained by two foreigners who were simply known as the "Wagn Bros". They played in several towns outside Colombo including Batticaloa and Jaffna. In addition to her musical activities, Mallika was a keen tennis player, and represented the school in the sport.

Notwithstanding her wide range of abilities, there was no doubt that the young Mallika was animated most of all by art. She notes that it was "doing things with her hands and fingers" that interested her the most. While at school, she attended Saturday classes at the Heywood School of Arts and Crafts where she learnt about crafting leather handbags and slippers, as well as beadwork.

In her later years at Visakha, Mallika aspired to become a doctor. Indeed, she could well have emulated her father had it not been for a personable young man whom she met whilst studiously preparing for the Higher School Certificate (HSC) examination, the results of which would have determined entry to medical school. Mallika met and fell in love with Dr Piyasiri Hemachandra, a medical practitioner, who incidentally hailed from a family that owned and operated a jewellery business. It was during a family holiday in Tangalle that she met Piyasiri, who at the time was working at the local hospital. It did not take her too long to realise that she wanted to share her life with this young doctor. Abandoning her own aspirations of a medical career, she therefore left Visakha to marry Piyasiri. It was a decision that set her along a very different path, but one that she would never regret.

While preparations for the wedding were underway, Mallika explored her artistic inclinations by enrolling in a silver jewellery-making course at the YWCA in Colombo. Ms. Fran Hooker, an American lady who was residing in Sri Lanka at the time, facilitated the class. Here, she was quick to learn the intricacies of designing and making bracelets, necklaces, rings and earrings, some of which were set with Sri Lankan precious stones such as blue and yellow sapphires, rubies and alexandrite, and semi-precious stones such as garnets, amethysts, citrine, topaz and peridot.

Following their marriage in 1960, Mallika and Piyasiri resided at her family home in Horton Place. It was not long after the wedding that Fran, having noticed Mallika's extraordinary creativity in jewellery crafting, asked her talented student to assume the supervisory role of the class of about fifteen students. Mallika initially respectfully declined the offer, in consideration of her youthful age and newly married status. When she learned of Fran's imminent departure from Sri Lanka, however, she finally relented and agreed to run the class.

As it turned out, however, Mallika could only complete a few months at the YWCA because soon after undertaking her new role there, Piyasiri decided to pursue postgraduate medical studies in the UK. Thus the young couple left Sri Lanka in 1963 and based themselves in the vibrant city of London, where Piyasiri commenced studying for a Diploma in Psychiatry. While Piyasiri settled into his four year study program, Mallika insightfully seized the opportunity to acquire an international qualification that would complement her nascent interest in the design and creation of jewellery. She enrolled in a two-year course at the Central School of Arts & Crafts in Holborn, London and graduated in 1967 with a Diploma in Jewellery Design. The Central School was a forerunner of London's renowned Central Saint Martins College of Art and Design, which has produced many world-famous graduates, including the interior and furniture designer, Sir Terence Conran, and the fashion designer, Stella McCartney.

Not long after obtaining her Diploma from the Central School, Mallika found herself on a plane from London to Switzerland. Encouraged by Piyasiri to further her knowledge in the field, she travelled with him to the Swiss city of Biel/Bienne to enquire about a modern jewellery-making technique which was used to cut and facet gold and silver. In picturesque Biel/Bienne – which is located about halfway between Geneva and Zurich – they met personnel from Posalux Machine Company, the institution that manufactured the unique machine and trained students in its operation. Mallika recalls the manager of the company, not anticipating a female trainee, appeared rather confused when she began asking questions about the training course. The manager's misconception was only clarified by directly enquiring of Piyasiri "Are you joining the training course?" to which Piyasiri quite simply replied, "No, it is my wife."

Satisfied that the course would be a worthwhile endeavour, Mallika embarked on a bold and visionary mission of spending three months in Biel/Bienne to pursue it. Learning in a small group with two others, an American and a Cypriot, Mallika mastered the new jewellery-making technique with surprising ease. Upon completion of her training, she was a competent operator of the machine, and proficient in its service and maintenance. Confident of her newly acquired skills, and fascinated by the machine's novel features, Mallika decided to buy one for her use in Sri Lanka. The purchase was an expensive one but years later, she would realise that it was money very well spent.

After completion of their respective courses, the Hemachandras headed home in December 1967 and resumed residence in Colombo with Mallika's parents. Mallika's precious cargo of machinery arrived some months later and immediately thereafter, she began her business of producing faceted jewellery, believed to be the first of its kind in Sri Lanka. In 1968, she formally incorporated it as Mallika Hemachandra Limited, with herself as the Chairperson, sole designer and manufacturer. In hindsight, the creation of the company marked a critical turning point in her life and career. Yet at the time, it was simply a natural progression of an interest in jewellery-making which began as a hobby, developed into a skill, and finally, turned into an entrepreneurial venture.

Mallika's product range included hand-crafted jewellery as well as machine-manufactured items, all of which were made in the home. Before long, the demand for her products had expanded to the extent that she decided to hire a skilled worker, who was also accommodated at home.

She soon found herself searching for additional production space in order to cope with an increasing volume of sales. By then, Mallika was the mother of two young children and naturally, it was her foremost concern that she had easy access to them during working hours. She recalls her husband saying to her: "You can do what you want in your own home, even turn it upside down. Don't go anywhere – just work from home." So, rather than move her business to a different location, Mallika sensibly converted an area of the family home into a workshop and showroom. Besides, working at home meant that her mother's support was always readily available in addition to the domestic help. It was immensely heartening to know that the children were in safe care and only "a peek away" while she busily maintained her long working hours.

The happy Hemachandra family was surely and steadily establishing a comfortable and contented lifestyle when suddenly, in January 1977, tragedy struck. Mallika's life radically changed when her husband unexpectedly passed away. The Hemachandras' children were still young; their son Chandima was 14 years old and their daughter Chamindri, only 11. Mallika herself was left as a youthful widow of just 44 years. The sudden demise of her husband and the subsequent assumption of sole responsibility for their children was immensely traumatic for Mallika. During this tremendous personal upheaval, she turned fervently to her business of jewellery-making, partly as escapism but also acutely aware that the small venture she had begun for pleasure was now the family's sole livelihood and source of income. Immersing herself in an occupation that she genuinely enjoyed proved to be a positive force in dealing with the enormity of Piyasiri's untimely loss. Above all, she derived courage from her parents, whom she describes as "a tower of strength" during those exceptionally difficult and emotional years, and without whose support she feels she could not have coped.

With the benefit of a deeper commitment to her work and the support of her loved ones, Mallika Hemachandra Limited grew from strength to strength. Mallika's creative ability and expanding involvement in her trade placed her in contact with several distinguished persons. These included members of royalty, who of course are well known to be patrons of high-quality jewellery. Most memorably, she met with Her Majesty Queen Elizabeth and Prince Philip during their 1981 visit to Sri Lanka, when she was privileged to be invited to the President's House for a private showing of her jewellery to the royal couple. She was delighted that the Queen showed a genuine interest in her work and asked several questions about the production of her pieces, such as the making time and the gold content in particular items. Quite to her surprise, she was conversationally engaged with Her Majesty for almost an hour, for which she was later gently teased by some cabinet ministers in attendance, who jokingly remarked the Queen had spoken to her the longest!

She also had the good fortune of meeting the charming Empress Michiko of Japan in 1985. This rare opportunity arose when she, along with three other Sri Lankans, attended a conference in Tokyo as a member of the Zonta Club of Colombo – an organisation devoted to advancing the status of women and engaged in charitable and community related projects. At the gala dinner that followed the conclusion of the conference, they found to their sheer amazement that they were sitting at the same table as Empress Michiko herself!

From its modest beginnings as a hobby, Mallika's personal drive and commitment saw her jewellery business flourish into one of Sri Lanka's best-known enterprises. The company expanded from a factory and showroom at Horton Place aimed at the upper end of the market, selling bridal jewellery and exclusively designed items, to one catering to a broader, multi-generational market via eight strategic outlets in Colombo and other major towns. In the mid-1990s, Mallika Hemachandra Limited was relaunched as a bilateral venture, with Horton Exports (Pvt) Limited as the manufacturing entity and MHJ as the marketing arm.

Today, the two companies employ a total workforce of around 150 employees. Over 50 of these are skilled workers, including designers, craftsmen and senior sales staff, with the majority trained by Mallika and her daughter Chamindri. The Horton Place venue now serves as the primary showroom and design studio where larger jewellery sets as well as designer pieces are made, while a modern factory on the outskirts of Colombo in Hokandara manufactures the more routine and classical items sold via branch outlets.

A chance meeting with the Emir of Bahrain Sheikh Al Khalifa who attended the Non-Aligned Conference held in Sri Lanka in 1981, culminated in a business relationship that led to Mallika opening her first and only overseas outlet in Bahrain in 1984. Although Mallika did not establish branches elsewhere, orders began flowing in from other locations overseas – mostly in Europe – for custom-made jewellery.

Mallika recalls yet another interesting encounter during an ordinary afternoon of business at her Horton Place premises during the mid-eighties. It began when she was startled by the sound of police sirens outside, but before she had the chance to investigate this unusual disturbance, Sheikha Al Khalifa, wife of the Emir of Bahrain at the time, strode into the showrooms unannounced and flanked by bodyguards. Not having the slightest idea that such VIPs were visiting Sri Lanka at the time, Mallika was both stunned and flattered by the unexpected royal call.

Mallika is fortunate to have had close family members involved in the successful operation and expansion of her enterprise. Her daughter Chamindri, a member of the Chartered Institute of Management Accountants (CIMA), gave up her job as an accountant in the commercial sector to join the family business in 1992. Subsequently, Chamindri decided to acquire formal training in Italy and developed her own passion for the trade. Since then, a unique mother-daughter combination has worked to strengthen MHJ's creative talent. She has been responsible for opening seven of the eight countrywide branches and has embarked on theme-based projects of her own, including the recently launched African Safari Collection.

Chamindri and her husband Asanga Karunaratne are both directors of the companies and together, manage the factory at Hokandara.

Pendant by Mallika

Meanwhile, Mallika's son Chandima Hemachandra, though currently working as Head of Information Technology in the CFC Bank in Nairobi, serves on the Board of Directors in both establishments and oversees the Information Technology aspects of the entire business.

Much of Mallika's work has been showcased and promoted through national and international exhibitions, some of which have been in aid of charitable fundraising projects. In 1968, her jewellery was displayed at a charity exhibition co-organised with the wife of the French Ambassador to Sri Lanka at the time. The exhibition, held at the Alliance Française in Colombo was opened by Mrs J.R. Jayawardene, the then First Lady of Sri Lanka, with all proceeds being donated to several projects via the Lions Club of Colombo. Mallika also exhibits her products annually at *Facets* Sri Lanka, the country's leading international gem and jewellery show which has been held every year since 1991 at the Bandaranaike Memorial International Conference Hall or at a five-star hotel in Colombo. In addition, she participated in several one-off events, such as "Jewellery on Clothes," a week-end of fashion showcasing a local collection held at the Galle Face Hotel, Colombo in 2005. Mallika designed and made dresses which cleverly incorporated jewellery items that were studded with precious stones. In the same year, she co-sponsored the Miss Sri Lanka for Miss World contest and gifted a 22-carat gold necklace to the winner, crowning her with Mallika's own creation of a crown in white gold set with semi-precious stones.

In addition to her regular participation in local events, Mallika has attended many key exhibitions and fashion shows overseas, including in Bahrain, Hong Kong, Germany, Malaysia, Thailand, Switzerland, the USA (Las Vegas), and the UAE. She travelled to Australia in 1999 as a member of a government-sponsored trade delegation, where she participated in well-attended trade shows at the Hilton hotels in Sydney and Melbourne.

Beyond her business endeavours, Mallika has conscientiously carried out various civic activities which benefit others in her industry as well as the community at large. For three years from 1992 to 1995 she was President of the Sri Lanka Jewellery Manufacturing Exporters Association, during which time she compiled and published a compendium of technical terms that significantly helped those working in the industry.

With such a crowded day-to-day program, one would think that Mallika would be devoid of time to enjoy other pleasures of life. But not so! For many years, she undertook home catering orders for cakes and desserts, using the talent and know-how acquired from her very capable mother. Unsurprisingly, Mallika excelled in and immensely enjoyed the creative process of decorating cakes and making delectable desserts. Flower-arranging was another art which came naturally to her. Floral displays have long adorned her home and she would also often help friends with the table décor at their special functions. Mallika's wide range of artistic talents also encompasses oil painting which she engages in purely as a hobby.

To have overcome the tragedy of losing her husband at a young age, while foraying successfully into a highly competitive, male-dominated field where she cut a lonely female figure for many years, is admirable indeed. It was not easy to succeed in such an environment but Mallika was determined to be a recognised force in the closely guarded jewellery industry and never lost sight of her objective, despite opposition from unlikely quarters. She has been inspired in her life and work by Lee Kwan Yew, the founder of modern Singapore, who propelled a small and obscure country on to the world stage within a short period of time, and as well, by Nelson Mandela's struggle and personal sacrifices to attain a much larger goal. "This is a business created out of nothing," she states proudly, and rightly so.

So what does she believe are the ingredients for success? Mallika credits her accomplishments to an unwavering self-confidence in her abilities, which she maintained constantly in her quest to achieve. To those aspiring to enter the industry, she would advise that discipline, dedication and commitment are vital attributes and in particular, maintaining the high standards of quality required in the jewellery trade – a requirement which she succinctly describes as "following the proper path with no short cuts." Ethical standards are no less important. In her own words, "one must do an honest and perfect job and it is only then that people will come back to you."

Now well into her seventies and a grandmother of five, there is no serious indication yet that Mallika will retreat from the passionate journey that she successfully travelled for so many decades, even as she claims she is quietly easing herself from daily pressures. As she is assured of the capabilities of the next generation – in particular of Chamindri, Asanga and Chandima – to continue the family business, and she is still brimming with enthusiasm and creative ideas, there is no reason why she should!

Maureen Seneviratne at the ceremony to become PC, 1983

Maureen Seneviratne
Lawyer

It is difficult to imagine that, until just a few decades ago, the legal profession in Sri Lanka was the exclusive domain of men. There were no women to be seen within the judiciary, at the bar, or in government law departments. It was in this forbidding era that Maureen Seneviratne embarked on a career in the law, and with spectacular results. She became the first woman to be appointed a President's Counsel, and achieved a host of other 'firsts' – thereby paving the way for a generation of female lawyers to enter and succeed in their chosen profession.

Born and raised in Colombo, the young Maureen never thought of becoming a lawyer. Her father Edward Seneviratne was a chief accountant at Ceylon Government Railways and her mother, Florence Seneviratne, a housewife. As a schoolgirl, Maureen was an excellent athlete. She won colours in netball for six years running at Ladies' College, Colombo, was part of the netball team that won the coveted Westrop Shield, and was a member of the school relay team. More exceptionally, she was a gifted musician and in particular, an outstanding pianist. A recipient of numerous prizes and certifications, Maureen is a Fellow and a Licentiate of the Trinity College of Music, London, as well as a Licentiate of the Royal College of Music, London. She was also a 'Grade A artist' on Radio Ceylon, which regularly broadcast her performances of classical music during her school and university days. Thus it was natural that Maureen first aspired to a career in music, setting her sights on becoming a concert pianist. At that time, however – unlike the present – there was very little scope in Sri Lanka for those with musical talent, beyond becoming a music teacher.

It was only after Maureen passed her university entrance examinations that she decided to study law. She proceeded to the campus of the University of Ceylon at Peradeniya, earning her LLB (Bachelor of Laws) degree in 1954. After graduating, she entered the Law College in Colombo to take her final examinations to qualify as a practitioner. At the time, there was a division of professions in the law, between advocates (who appeared in court) and proctors (who did notarial work). In order to take oaths as an advocate, one had to pass the final examination and then serve an apprenticeship. Maureen passed the examination for advocates with flying colours – achieving first class honours

– and after serving a six-month apprenticeship under the eminent lawyer N.K. Choksy QC, she took oaths, thereby becoming the first woman to qualify as an advocate in Sri Lanka.

No sooner had she qualified as an advocate, Maureen was awarded a prestigious Smith-Mundt scholarship by the State Department of the United States government. The scholarship took her to Yale University, where she won admission to pursue a LLM (Master's of Law) degree at the renowned Yale Law School. There were just two female students in the LLM class of about twenty students; Maureen, and one other young woman from Oxford. The year she spent abroad unfolded a wealth of new experiences and friendships. It was at Yale Law School that Maureen got her first taste of advocacy when she took part in its long-established "Thurman Arnold Prize" moot court competition. Although she did not win the prize, Maureen placed well and recalls that she was the first Asian woman to take part in the competition, just as she was the first Sri Lankan woman to obtain a LLM degree.

Maureen had the good fortune to meet wonderful people at Yale, several of whom she still counts among her closest friends. They include Anna Diggs Taylor, now a federal court judge in the United States, Alice Henkin, a well-known human rights activist, and the American Ambassador Ulric Haynes, all of whom were her contemporaries at Yale. She speaks venerably of her former professors, whom she found to be refreshingly different from anyone who had taught her before. At Yale, she recounts, the professors were really friends of the students – they were so distinguished in their fields and yet incredibly down-to-earth. Students could freely go and discuss issues with them no matter how busy they were. Her professors at Yale included the judge and scholar Jerome Frank, as well as Myres McDougal, one of the world's most renowned professors of international law. Fittingly with her love of music, Maureen also became friends with the Dean of the School of Music and eminent organist, Professor Luther M. Noss, and his wife Osea. Professor and Mrs Noss stayed with her when they visited Ceylon in the 1970s; and Maureen too stayed at the Noss' home when she later returned to New Haven to attend a celebration at Yale Law School to mark the 80th birthday of Professor Myres McDougal, an event to which she was personally invited by the honouree himself.

Maureen's professors urged her to remain at Yale after completing her LLM in order to pursue a doctorate. But further studies were not to be. She had a wonderful year in the United States, which to this day she admires as a country where people are judged on their abilities rather than on their status or connections. The terms of

As a young lawyer

Maureen after her graduation

the Smith-Mundt scholarship, however, required her to return to Sri Lanka. And although she was sad to leave the magical intellectual environs of Yale, Maureen was also eager to come back to Sri Lanka to be with her parents and to finally commence the practice of law.

When asked why she was so keen to practise, Maureen's reply is profound. She reveals that she wished to practise law "for the simple reason, that even as a child, I revolted against injustice and discrimination". It is clear that Maureen was not motivated – as many aspiring lawyers are – by a love of debating or courtroom drama, or the pursuit of money or fame. Rather, she was driven by a yearning to see justice done. Maureen had suffered as a schoolgirl at the hands of one of her principals, whom Maureen recalls as a harsh disciplinarian who did not treat her fairly. To Maureen, the injustices she endured were only remedied under the leadership of another school principal – a wonderful lady named Miss Mabel Simon – who guided her through her final years of study at Ladies' College. She recounts that Miss Simon was an inspirationally fair-minded principal, who treated all students alike, and who was always ready to listen to the students' side of a story. The exemplary stewardship of Miss Simon brought long-awaited joy to Maureen's schooldays, and enabled her to forget her earlier unhappiness. Maureen elucidates that it was her experiences as a schoolgirl which really made her take to law. She was moved to take up the cause of the underdog and those experiencing inequity because she could identify with their situation and knew what a difference a just hand could make.

Maureen commenced legal practice immediately upon her return to Sri Lanka from the United States. It was not, however, an easy transition to make. As the only female advocate, she felt isolated in the profession when she joined, so much so that she was petrified to enter even the law library! When she began practising, she had no robing room to use – indeed, not even a toilet. Her senior, N.K. Choksy QC, spoke about Maureen's predicament to a judge, Justice L.B. de Silva, who kindly told Maureen that she could robe in his room provided he was not using it at the time. She appreciated this gesture but of course, it was neither a satisfactory nor a permanent solution. She had nowhere to robe when Justice de Silva was using his room and naturally, he could not be expected to offer his room to every other female advocate who would join the profession. Hence Maureen fought, in the face of immense opposition, for a separate robing room for women. When one was finally allocated, it was small, dark and unventilated – so unappealing that Maureen vividly describes it as "like the black hole of Calcutta." It was not until the 1980s that the full fruits of Maureen's early struggles for separate facilities for women were realised, when an ample robing room for their use was built into the new superior courts complex in Hulftsdorp, Colombo.

The difficulties that Maureen experienced as a woman lawyer were not limited to obtaining suitable court facilities. In common with other working women of her time, she had to contend with idle gossip and falsehoods about her professional and personal life. When asked how she bore the opposition, slurs, and other burdens of being a woman in her chosen profession, Maureen cites her faith in God and the tremendous encouragement she received from those who supported her career. She remarks that she was very fortunate that she apprenticed under such an outstanding senior as the late N.K. Choksy QC, and appreciatively remembers how kind and helpful he was to her work. Indeed, recalls Maureen, Mr Choksy came to be referred to as the guardian angel of women lawyers. She readily acknowledges that she owes so much of her success to him. Maureen was also fortunate in having other stalwarts of the Bar to steer her and in particular, she is grateful to D.S. Jayawickrama QC, H.V. Perera QC, C.V. Ranawaka, George Chitty QC and P. Navaratnarajah QC. With the steadfast support of these leading lawyers, she was able to stand up to the hostility she had to face from certain male members and powerful sections of the Bar. But for these "incredibly decent, kind" men, notes Maureen, she may have given up.

Of course, Maureen also drew strength from her own family. Her parents wisely counselled her not to be concerned with what others said. They explained to Maureen that she had nothing to worry about in her career if she always acted to the best of her ability and with propriety. Maureen had two brothers – both lawyers – and two sisters, and was especially close to her brother Eardley Seneviratne whom she describes as a lawyer "much sought after by rich and poor alike". Eardley was another guiding force in Maureen's life and career and his recent demise has left her with an irreplaceable void.

Maureen's career at the Bar has spanned many different facets of the law. She is, first and foremost, a skilled advocate who is highly sought after in civil (i.e. non-criminal) cases. Maureen appeared in the landmark case of *Canekeratne v Canekeratne* (1968) where she represented a woman who had been deserted by her husband. The case was fiercely contested and the husband was represented by an eminent silk but ultimately, Maureen succeeded in persuading the Supreme Court to recognise new legal rights of a deserted wife. The decision in *Canekeratne v Canekeratne* has since been cited innumerable times by lawyers and judges in subsequent matrimonial cases. Maureen also appeared in some major land and tenancy cases throughout the 1960s and 1970s, including in the case of *Charlotte Perera v Thambiah and Another* (1983) before a full bench of the Supreme Court. She remarks with an understandable sense of satisfaction that these were all cases in which she sought to remedy a real injustice.

It is to Maureen's great dismay that, even today, the poor in Sri Lanka have little or no access to justice because litigation is prohibitively expensive and legal procedures so cumbersome. Like many lawyers with a concern for social justice, Maureen has acted *pro bono* for impoverished clients many a time, but the total number of cases in which lawyers waive or reduce their fees is drastically insufficient to ensure equal access to justice. She is glad that Sinhala-speaking people can at least now argue their cases in their mother tongue, a development which she views as a "great step forward" for the participation of the poor and underprivileged in the legal system.

As a junior lawyer, Maureen quickly became known as a highly skilled and sought-after advocate, both within and beyond the legal community. She successfully took on many memorable cases, and reflects that she was lucky to appear before excellent judges who were receptive to her arguments and encouraged her tremendously. Eventually, Maureen received the ultimate accolade for a practising lawyer during the tenure of Neville Samarakoon as Chief Justice, when she was appointed as a President's Counsel in 1983. She thus became the first woman in Sri Lanka to be given silk. In receiving this honour, Maureen felt that all her previous trials and tribulations had been worth it, that she was duly rewarded for her years of travail. She is particularly gratified to have been made a President's Counsel during the judicial reign of Neville Samarakoon, whom she regards as one of the most upright, able men with enormous integrity and courage, and who was never unduly influenced, politically or otherwise. It was unfortunate that neither of her parents lived to see this glorious moment of her career, for Maureen knows how proud they would have been of their daughter.

Her renown as a practising lawyer did not prevent Maureen from successfully taking on other professional responsibilities. During the 1970s, she was appointed to chair an important committee – popularly known as the rent committee – which was tasked with considering and recommending amendments to the rent law under the government of Sirimavo Bandaranaike. The committee made many far-reaching recommendations, which were implemented and

In court dress as a President's Counsel

provided substantial relief to tenants. She faced a difficult time during her term as chairman of the rent committee, when one leading daily newspaper published defamatory material about her. Maureen courageously fought back and sued the newspaper; with the dedicated representation of her counsel, Mr P. Navaratnarajah QC, she was successful in winning damages. When the newspaper appealed to the Supreme Court, she prevailed in the appeal case as well. As she justly explains, she sued not for the money but to clear her reputation. She further elucidates that one's reputation means everything whether you are a professional or not, and she felt compelled to take action because it is an unfortunate fact that many people are always prepared to believe the worst of others.

It was also in the 1970s that Maureen was appointed Chairman of the Board of Review, which oversaw the Rent Board. She found this to be a most enjoyable experience, not least because she had the opportunity to lead an excellent board of several other members. During the same decade, Maureen was selected to serve on a panel of the Industrial Court and as an Examiner of the Council of Legal Education, both appointments which she held for about three years. Maureen notes that she was the first woman to be appointed to each of these positions.

Given the nature of her work, Maureen's career did not carry a substantial international dimension. After all, each country has its own laws and so practising civil lawyers do not normally travel and work abroad in the same way that say, engineers, accountants or professors might do. Maureen did, however, attend law conferences overseas, including a LawAsia conference held in Hong Kong in 1980, and comments that she benefited from such interactions, since she was able to meet fine lawyers abroad with whom she could exchange ideas. In addition, she has never ceased to maintain contact with the people she met during the year in the United States, whom she still counts as her closest friends.

Perhaps Maureen's most fascinating international experience was her visit to the former Soviet Union in the 1970s, as part of a Sri Lankan delegation to that country. The delegation comprised a handful of individuals from different walks of life – among whom Maureen was the only lawyer – who were taken to cities and places across the vast extent of the Soviet Union, including Leningrad, Moscow, and Uzbekistan. Maureen was so impressed with what she witnessed during her trip that when she returned to Sri Lanka and spoke glowingly about it, her friends jokingly labelled her a communist stooge. She makes clear that she did not see the objectionable aspects of the Soviet Union which people so frequently discussed, so she could not speak of those. But of course, when she stated this point to her friends, they would say "ah, you wouldn't have been taken to those places!"

In any event, Maureen recalls that in every place that she visited, she saw the most impressive buildings and met wonderfully agreeable people. She was taken by the fact that people looked so happy and contented, and especially, by the absence of unnecessary luxuries and the lack of a distinction between rich and poor. During her trip, she made an interesting visit to the home of the then First Secretary at the Soviet Embassy in Sri Lanka whom she recollects was a Mr Vinick. Although he lived in one of the largest houses in Colombo's exclusive Rosmead Place, she was struck by the fact that his home in Russia was a simple two-roomed house – with modern facilities, but modest nonetheless. From what Maureen saw, everyone in the Soviet Union had equal opportunities, including to the country's astonishingly rich cultural life. She cheerfully remembers that one could visit the famed Bolshoi Theatre for merely one or two roubles!

Travel and culture remain an important part of Maureen's life, albeit now for personal pleasure rather than for official or professional reasons. Though she continues to practise law, she made a conscious decision several years

Maureen playing the piano at home in Colombo, 2011

ago to reduce her workload so that she could see more of the world. She normally does one significant trip abroad each year, usually by way of an organised tour, which she enjoys because of the many delightful people she meets on such tours. When asked how she likes to spend her free time when not travelling, Maureen mentions both reading and listening to good music. It is a matter of regret to her that she is no longer a serious pianist – she plays occasionally nowadays, but not in the manner she used to. Her free time is still limited, however, because she still works from her chambers at her home in Colombo and, as she remarks, has no plans to retire! Though the lifestyle of a practising lawyer is not an easy one – it involves, for example, seeing clients and preparing for cases in the evening – she intends to work for as long as she can.

When asked what advice she would give to young women who are considering entering the legal profession, Maureen is adamant that, in this era, they do not need much advice. She points to the fact that there are now countless women lawyers, many of whom hold senior positions in the public and private sectors and several of whom are well-regarded advocates. In terms of gender equity, the legal profession today is a far cry from what it was when Maureen joined it over half a century ago. The only counsel she would offer to women in any profession is to be cautious in what they do and say, so as not to provide their opponents fodder for maligning them in any way. For as Maureen observes, "Any woman in public life or who is successful has to guard her reputation." At the same time, if she does find herself under fire, she must have the courage to fight back.

A final note of wisdom which Maureen offers, to both men and women who succeed in their chosen fields, is on the need for humility. She recalls that the judges whom she appeared before as a junior, her senior Mr Choksy, and her professors at Yale, were all amazingly modest men with incredible humility. She learned from them that the more successful you are in life, the humbler you must be. As she puts it "You cannot be suspended in mid-air all your life. Someday you have to come down." These are sage words indeed and yet, it is difficult for any objective outsider to describe Maureen's work and legacy in modest terms. Those who have followed in her footsteps have rightly recognised Maureen as a trailblazer for future generations of women lawyers in Sri Lanka. Not long ago, Shanthi Eva Wanasundera PC, Additional Solicitor General and one of the few female advocates after Maureen to have been appointed a President's Counsel, encapsulated her impact in the following words: "From a career point of view, I think now the path is paved for many females aspiring to reach higher goals in the legal profession. In this regard, we must not forget Ms. Maureen Seneviratne, Sri Lanka's first lady President's Counsel, who set an example for all of us proving what women are capable of."

Premala Sivaprakasapillai Sivasegaram at the Structural Designs Office in Transworks House, Dept. of Buildings, Colombo, circa 1981

Premala Sivaprakasapillai Sivasegaram
Engineer

In many ways, Premala Sivaprakasapillai's childhood was typical of other girls raised during the 1940s. The young Premala enjoyed playing with dolls and doll houses. She appreciated dancing and music, having commenced dancing classes even before she began schooling. Her mother, Leelamani was keen that her only daughter be exposed to such arts at an early age, perhaps in anticipation of Premala becoming an accomplished housewife. Premala, however, came to have very different aspirations, which were rare for girls at that time. Deciding to pursue an engineering degree in her teens, Premala eventually gained the distinction of becoming the first woman to graduate from the Faculty of Engineering of what was then the University of Ceylon.

Premala recalls that her parents never stood in the way of her studies or of her budding interest in engineering. Around the age of five, she turned her attention to the Meccano set that her brothers played with. "I loved playing with my dolls and enjoyed dancing and music but I found the Meccano set challenging," remarks Premala.

Her fascination with the Meccano set may have been considered a rather unusual preoccupation for a girl of Premala's age at that time. Still, who could have guessed that she would one day be involved in such a highly visible and notable project as the structural design of Sri Lanka's busy international airport?

The youngest of three children, Premala was born on 21 April 1942 at her grand uncle's residence, situated within the Jaffna Fort in the northern city of Jaffna. It was around the time when families were evacuated from Colombo to escape wartime air raids. In her early years, Premala lived with her parents and two elder brothers in government housing quarters in Longden Place, Colombo, though the family travelled twice a year to Jaffna to visit relatives and attend the family temple ceremony. A fairly conservative family, the Sivaprakasapillais did not allow her to venture out much socially and in her childhood, Premala was quite happy to entertain herself at home with her toys.

In retrospect, her early fascination with the Meccano set was perhaps unsurprising. After all, Premala was born to a family of engineers. Her civil servant father, T. Sivaprakasapillai, was the first Sri Lankan engineer to work in the Colombo Harbour. As a child, she would visit the harbour with her father and be intrigued by the heavy engineering equipment whirring at the site. With both her brothers studying engineering, Premala recalls wanting to see if she could study it too – more for fun than simply to follow her brothers' footsteps!

Premala commenced school in the nursery of Ladies' College, Colombo. Her mother ensured she attended dancing classes as an extra-curricular activity, first in western ballet and subsequently in the traditional South Asian dance forms of *Bharata Natyam* and *Manipuri*. But Premala shone most in her academic studies, winning the class prize for first place in several years throughout school. By the time she was fourteen, her heart was set on becoming an engineer. "No one pushed me. The drive to do well came from within," recollects Premala, who was also a school prefect and enjoyed her time at school. Yet she is grateful to all her dedicated school teachers, including the visiting teachers Mr George Ondaatje and Mr Maurice de Silva, as well as to Miss Mabel Simon, who was the Principal of Ladies' College at the time and who encouraged Premala throughout her schooldays.

At the GCE O-level Premala faced one of her few academic disappointments. The pressure of a public examination weighing on her, she did not sleep well the night before and failed to live up to her expectations of obtaining a distinction in her favourite subject, mathematics; ending up with a credit instead. Two years later, however, she overcame this initial disappointment with brilliant results at the university entrance examination. Premala achieved distinctions in all four of her subjects – Physics, Chemistry, Pure Mathematics and Applied Mathematics – a result that won her an Exhibition (awarded for outstanding achievement) from the University of Ceylon.

Notwithstanding such brilliance in the entrance examination, the Dean of the Faculty of Engineering, upon learning of Premala's application for admission to pursue a degree in Civil Engineering, sincerely believing it was not a suitable field for women, tried to dissuade her from embarking on this path. He suggested to her father, who at the time was a fellow faculty member, that she should choose another discipline instead. The fact that her family was fairly conservative did not make it any easier for Premala either, even though some of her aunts had attended university and Premala's enthusiasm for tertiary studies had been spurred by listening to their interesting stories about *varsity* life. Thankfully, Premala's parents did not interfere with her plans and aspirations, trusting in their daughter's judgement.

Being a determined young woman undeterred by external influences, Premala entered a hitherto male-dominated domain in 1960 by enrolling in the Faculty of Engineering at the University of Ceylon's Colombo campus. "Because the two lecture halls were roofed with galvanized iron sheets, the building was known as the *takarang* faculty!" she recalls laughingly.

Premala graced the faculty's simply constructed buildings as the only woman in her year. Nonetheless, she did not feel any gender differentiation. On the contrary, her fellow engineering students interacted well with her, accepting her as their equal; though it was not unusual at the university to hear heckling and hooting whenever a group of girls walked into the lecture hall. The initiation practice of "ragging", a harsh practice though not nearly as cruel as it is these days, was also routinely inflicted on first year undergraduates. Fortunately, Premala was never a victim of any unsavoury acts. "I think I may have been spared because my father was a faculty member and perhaps too because my brothers were at the time seniors in the same faculty," she notes.

Throughout her university days, Premala continued with her dancing. It was a great form of relaxation from her studies, especially as she was working hard towards gaining first class honours. Both her brothers had gained first class honours in their engineering degrees and Premala recalls her friends and teachers saying she must do it too! Premala did not let herself down, nor anyone else. She graduated in October 1964 with first class honours and was awarded a Ceylon Government University Scholarship, in what was to be the last batch of engineering students to graduate from the Colombo campus before the faculty was relocated to the picturesque campus at Peradeniya.

Prior to taking up her scholarship, Premala spent a year at Peradeniya as an instructor. It so happened that an ex-colleague from her undergraduate days, Sivanandam Sivasegaram, was also at the Peradeniya campus at the same time, having taken up an assistant lecturer post in mechanical engineering. A casual friendship that originated during their undergraduate years in Colombo blossomed into romance and during the same year they became engaged. But with Premala due to pursue doctoral studies at a university overseas under the scholarship and Sivasegaram bound by a two-year term in his position at Peradeniya, their marriage plans had to be deferred. Besides, Premala's father was keen that she completed her doctorate before marriage, particularly since some of her aunts had entered university, then married and did not complete their degrees!

Thus, Premala set off alone in 1965 to pursue a doctorate at the University of Oxford, where she was based at Somerville College. Since she had not been away from home before, she felt comfortable residing in a women-only college as Somerville was then. It was a challenging time for Premala but she derived much guidance and support from her doctoral supervisor Dr John Renton, also an engineer. She remembers how one day at college she was handed a cumbersome old-style calculator by her senior lecturer. "You can carry it. You are an engineer!" he exclaimed. This was a moment of realisation for Premala – that in her field she was expected to be tough.

She often experienced loneliness being the only woman doing a post-graduate engineering degree, but she did not allow her feelings to dampen her spirits, recalling Oxford as an enjoyable and interesting experience for more reasons than her studies. The late sixties was an era of vibrant fashions and she could see colourful swirling designs replacing the drab tones of brown and grey, as well as the gradual disappearance of long skirts!

While writing her thesis on structural engineering, Premala commenced employment with the UK Ministry of Public Building & Works in 1968. Based in Oxford, her three years in the famous university town passed by quickly and she submitted her thesis in January 1969, to obtain a DPhil (Oxon).

In 1966, Sivasegaram, after completing his two-year term at Peradeniya, joined Premala in England and began studying for his PhD at Imperial College, London. No sooner were they reunited, arranging their wedding became a priority after his arrival. They were married in London in December 1968, in what Premala describes as "a typical Hindu wedding ceremony – improvised of course!"

Their son Manimaaran was born in London the following November – Premala courageously working until a week before his birth. Looking back, Premala was glad she finished her doctoral thesis when she did, as she feels it would have

Premala engaging in traditional dance

been challenging for both parents to be studying for a doctorate at the same time.

Meanwhile, the Public Works Department (PWD) of Sri Lanka was enquiring as to when she would be returning to discharge her five years of compulsory government service. To honour her commitments, Premala dutifully returned to Sri Lanka in April 1970 with her infant son. After completing his PhD, Sivasegaram followed them to Sri Lanka three months later. Premala's first posting back in her home country was as an assistant to the District Engineer, Kandy, of the Buildings Department. Sivasegaram recommenced his academic position at Peradeniya and the young family took up residence in the historic city of Kandy.

In the District Engineer's office, Premala was responsible for building maintenance as well as new constructions. Premala recalls her first day on the job when she received a telephone call from the Government Agent. She accepted the call enthusiastically only to hear the voice at the other end of the telephone asking her to check a malfunctioning toilet in his home! Fortunately for her, the District Engineer, an experienced and considerate person named Mr Dias, said to her "you need not go," saving her from what would have been an unwelcome situation. After gaining two years' experience assisting the District Engineer, Premala had the required practical experience to obtain membership at the Institute of Engineers, Sri Lanka.

In 1972, Premala moved with her son to Colombo to take up the position of Structural Engineer in the Buildings Department's Design Office. This was during Mrs Sirimavo Bandaranaike's era as Prime Minister, when much of the construction work was sourced locally so as to curb foreign exchange outflows. The years preceding the 1976 Non-Aligned Conference required several major projects to be completed, including the extension and refurbishment of the renamed Bandaranaike International Airport just outside Colombo. Premala remembers this as a particularly interesting and high-profile project, and to have been a member of a purely local team that completed the project on time provided her great pride and satisfaction.

Around the same period, she was also involved in the structural design of the Police Headquarters in the Colombo Fort. She remembers this as a unique building comprising twelve stories on a raft foundation on the land side, with a three-storied portion spanning the road and founded on piles on the sea side – forming a sort of arch over the road where cars passed by. The National Library and the National Archives, both of which are on Colombo's Independence Avenue, were some of the other notable buildings she co-designed.

In recognition of her abilities, Premala was promoted in 1978 to Chief Structural Engineer, a position she held until 1985. By the time she completed her tenure, the Design Office was respected as a solid training ground for young graduates, some of whom came from England, India and Russia to gain design experience in its bustling quarters.

While at the Buildings Department, Premala had the opportunity to travel to several countries to present papers, attend conferences and undergo further training. At the invitation of the Australian government, she jointly presented a paper in 1980 at the First International Conference of Technology for Development, held in Canberra. During this visit, she also travelled to the James Cook University in Townsville, Queensland and to the Building Research Institute in Sydney. The USA, Sweden and India are some of the other countries she was fortunate to visit in her professional capacity.

In 1985 Premala was presented with a fascinating opportunity. She was selected as a consultant to the Commonwealth Fund for Technical Cooperation to work with the Ministry of Education in Barbados, an appointment which further underscored her talents. At that time, her husband and son were in England with Manimaaran pursuing his education there. Thus Premala, who was also keen to leave Sri Lanka following the country's 1983 ethnic violence, proceeded to Barbados on her own.

For Premala, travelling around this picturesque little island of 431 square kilometres, designing new schools, was a unique experience. She lived in a beautiful apartment in a resort complex surrounded by a golf course which made her feel as if she was on an extended holiday rather than a working assignment. The hotel was frequented by the visiting international and West Indian cricket teams giving her the opportunity to see some of the famous cricketers such as Joel Garner and Michael Holding. The relaxed ambience undoubtedly helped her get through the heavy workload and life away from her family.

After completing her contract in Barbados in 1988, Premala joyously rejoined Sivasegaram and Manimaaran in London, where she proceeded to study for an MSc in Management at Imperial College. In fact, Imperial College appears to be the *de facto* family university, with many of her family members having walked its great halls. Premala's father was a graduate from Imperial, and it is where Sivasegaram, and one of Premala's brothers, earned their doctorates. In 1988, Manimaaran entered as an undergraduate as a third generation Imperial student in Premala's family, later graduating as a chemical engineer in the family tradition. Coincidentally, whilst his son and wife were studying there, Sivasegaram was Principal Research Fellow at Imperial!

When Premala completed her MSc in 1989, the British economy was slowing, making it difficult to secure employment at the time. Yet, she managed to obtain the position of Senior Professional Technical Officer in the Property Services Agency (previously the Ministry of Public Building and Works) the following year. She was responsible for project management and structural design of various buildings for the Ministry of Defence. Shortly after she joined, the organisation was privatized and became part of the Tarmac group.

During the height of the recession in 1995, Premala left Tarmac following a restructuring of that company, and proceeded to join London's Camden Council as Senior Engineer. Her experience in design stood her in good stead to secure this position during a severe economic downturn. "Not everyone was so lucky," she says.

In 1997, after a seven-year stint in the UK civil service, Premala and Sivasegaram decided it was time to return to Sri Lanka, primarily for personal reasons; Premala's parents were ageing, and she felt a need to be closer to them. In Sri Lanka, she joined the Open University of Sri Lanka as Senior Lecturer. Premala welcomed this new professional endeavour, for as she comments, "I always had a desire to teach and so this was a great opportunity."

Premala is a woman who has sought to contribute to society through her profession. While working in London in the 1960s, she joined the Women's Engineering Society, a nationwide organisation that promoted engineering amongst women in the UK. As an active member, she visited schools and participated in seminars for schoolgirls to stimulate their interest in engineering. She was also editor of Sri Lanka's Institute of Engineers' Quarterly Journal from 1977 to 1980. More recently, she has researched and written a book on the *History of Engineering in Sri Lanka*, a volume published for the Institute's Centenary Celebration in January 2006.

In Sri Lanka, Premala did not feel disadvantaged just because she was a woman. Her work was always recognised and respected and she received her due promotions. Unfortunately she is unable to say the same about England. She felt it was harder to prove herself and gain recognition in the sixties, possibly because of sexual and/or racial bias at the time (especially with few women engineers around), whilst her age was probably not in her favour in the latter years of her career. Indeed, Premala has encountered tough situations in her professional life, which is not surprising given that she was a

Colombo Archives, one of the buildings Premala was involved in constructing; (inset) Premala at a London building site, circa 1995

pioneer female engineer. Sensitive to the fact that being a woman, refusal would have exacerbated sexual prejudice, never did she say "no, I cannot," no matter how challenging the task.

Notwithstanding any external pressures she may have felt, Premala thoroughly enjoys her profession and has absolutely no regrets having chosen such a challenging field. "I feel a great sense of satisfaction when a building I have designed is completed. It is a visible achievement and a thrilling experience," she observes. It was also a career that opened many doors for her to travel and see places in Sri Lanka and overseas. Knowing that some of her clients may have saved money because of her advice instils in her a sense of happiness, and she feels gratified having imparted her knowledge to so many young people. Of course, she was fortunate to have a supportive family who made it possible to achieve what she did in the academic and professional fields, as well as to balance her personal and family life.

Her advice to other women aspiring to be civil engineers is that if they are keen, willing to undergo some hardship, and lucky to get the right jobs, it is a wonderful career. But equally, she cautions: "Do not do it unless you are really keen. Just because one is good at mathematics, and teachers steer you in that direction, does not necessarily mean engineering is the career for you". Evidently though, engineering was the right path for Premala, having led her to a groundbreaking and fulfilling professional life.

Premala at her graduation, 1964

Premila Diwakara at her graduation ceremony, 1959

Premila Diwakara
Police Officer

Premila Diwakara led a highly successful career in the police force, a field which many still perceive as an occupation reserved for men. Appointed as a woman police constable (WPC) in 1958, Premila forged through the ranks of Sri Lanka's police force to become its first female Senior Superintendent of Police in 1999. Her success is a testament to the enthusiasm of her youth, her ongoing determination, and her joy in serving her country.

Premila hails from Madurawala, a village close to the town of Horana, near Colombo. She was born in June 1939 as the younger of two sisters. The sisters grew up under the care of their mother, a housewife, and their father, a contractor and farmer. Both Premila and her sister were educated in the village school until grade 5 and thereafter, to ensure they learned English, both girls were sent to Sri Palee College, Horana. Sri Palee was a co-educational school and Premila was boarded at its hostel from grade 8 onwards.

At Sri Palee, Premila was an energetic and (in her own words) "mischievous" schoolgirl. It was there that she began her love of sports and of athletics in particular – a passion which she would continue to pursue during her years in the police force. Premila started her sporting activities at the age of 11, participated in several inter-school, inter-province, Western Province and 'All Island' sporting meets, and became the school's Games Captain.

While Premila's mother encouraged her daughters to enter into the fields of teaching or nursing, Premila had somewhat different career aspirations. There were no police officers in the family, but as a teenager, Premila happened to see one of Sri Lanka's first women police constables during a weekend visit home from the Sri Palee hostel. By chance, the family of the WPC lived near Premila's home in Madurawala and Premila saw her while she was reporting to the local police station, as was customary for police officers when they took leave to go back home. It was at that moment that Premila was taken with the idea of joining the police force, prompting her to think, "Oh, I'd love to be a policewoman!"

While still at Sri Palee, Premila made her first application to join the police force. In 1957, she saw a gazette notification calling for applications for the post of WPC. Unfortunately, Premila's application was rejected – as the required minimum age of applicants was 18 years, and

Premila was then only 17 years and 6 months. Undeterred, Premila applied once again in 1958, during her A-level year and having reached the age of eighteen. This time, she was successful in being called for an interview.

Premila's recollections about the selection process reveal her bold character, which was apparent even in her youth. The first interview was held in Colombo and as it happened, Premila had never been to Colombo. Hence when she was informed that the interview would be held at the Depot Police, Bambalapitiya, she did not know how she would even reach there. Premila could not ask her parents to take her to the interview, as she was sure that they would vehemently oppose the idea of her becoming a police officer. The only family member that she told about the interview was her sister, who teased her about applying to the police force and said she would never be selected. So Premila told the Sri Palee warden that she was going home for an urgent matter and unbeknownst to her parents, proceeded to make her own way to Colombo, accompanied by a friend.

When she finally arrived at the Depot Police in Colombo for the interview and saw all her fellow applicants, Premila initially thought her application was a big mistake. She seemed so small-made compared to all the other women! Nevertheless, she fared very well in the interview. Premila had brought with her all the sports certificates she had been awarded in school and the interviewers were impressed by her sports activities. The chair of the panel even joked that it would take an entire day for them to wade through all of her certificates! In addition to demonstrating her sporting abilities, Premila showed them evidence of other extra-curricular activities, such as first aid. At the end of the interview, she was delighted to hear that she would be called for the next interview.

Premila was well on her way to becoming one of just fourteen WPCs selected from approximately 14,000 women applicants that year. The letter inviting her to the second stage of the selection process was sent to Premila's home address, and thus her parents came to know of her application to become a WPC. This sparked intense discussions between Premila and her mother as to the suitability of a career in the police force. Premila's mother was adamant that after all her parents had spent on her education, Premila should become a teacher or a nurse, which in that era were regarded as the most respectable professions for a woman. Her father was less perturbed, seeing no reason why Premila should not join the police force, if she was prepared for what such a career would entail. In any event, Premila convinced her mother that although it was unlikely she would be selected, she should at least try. The second stage of the selection process involved a medical test for filaria and required applicants to stay overnight in Colombo. With her parents' permission, she went to Colombo accompanied by a cousin, stayed overnight at a relative's home in Slave Island, and returned the following day after the filaria test.

A week passed before Premila received another letter, this time inviting her to come for a written test and a medical check-up. She attended this last stage of the selection process and shortly thereafter, at the end of September 1958, she received what she had long awaited: a letter of selection as a WPC with a direction to report to the police training school (now the Police College) in Kalutara on 1 October 1958. Once again, she had to convince her mother to permit her to proceed. Her mother reiterated her desire to see Premila continue her studies and try to become a teacher, but finally relented when Premila pleaded to be allowed to go. To her dismay, the selection letter contained a long list of items that she was required to bring to the training school. Premila did not have the funds to purchase these. As her parents were not fully supportive of her career plans, she asked relatives and friends for money to buy the required items and promised to repay them when she had the funds.

The police training school involved intensive training and trainees were required to live on-campus. Premila was one of 14 women out of 700 new recruits; women underwent the same training as men. She completed her six month training at the police training school in April 1959.

Just once, at the very beginning of her career, Premila was tempted to abandon her foray into the police force. Midway through her police training, she was offered the position of a clerk with a company at Ratnapura – a job that she had applied for earlier. Premila's mother delightedly brought Premila the appointment letter, convinced that Premila would leave the police training school for a white-collar position. And indeed, after receiving this job offer, Premila herself thought she should leave. Her superiors, however, were adamant that she should not abandon her ambition to be a police officer. They assured Premila that she would have a good future as an officer, and insisted that she was much more suited to be in the police force than at a desk job. Premila reflected on their words of encouragement, initially informing her mother that she would think about the job offer at Ratnapura and write back to the company the following week. Finally, Premila decided to keep pursuing her dreams. She diplomatically explained to her mother that, as she was now halfway through her training, it would be best to complete it and she could then decide upon her eventual job after graduation.

Premila's first appointment upon graduation was as a WPC with the Harbour Police. She was assigned there because she was an English-speaker and during that era, most tourists arrived by sea. After four years with the Harbour Police, she was assigned to the Colombo City Traffic Police in 1963, which brought different experiences. She worked tirelessly with schools and schoolchildren; teaching road safety, and conducting road rules awareness programs, including guidance on how to cross roads.

As Premila was advancing in her chosen career, the time came to also determine more personal matters. She had had a steady boyfriend from her schooldays and they wished to get married. In preparation for married life, Premila thought it wise to move to a civilian position. Thus in 1964, she began working in the fingerprints section of the Criminal Investigation Department (CID) in Torrington Square, Colombo. Premila and her husband, Mr Eddie Premasiri Guruge, were married in 1965. Her husband is a planter, who worked in the Galle area both before and after their marriage.

Premila's husband has always supported her career in the police force. Just once, early on in their marriage when Premila was based at the CID in Colombo and he was near Galle, he suggested that she leave the police force because of the separation it involved between them. Premila responded in a way that both overcame the issue of separation and reflected her desire to stay in the police force. In 1965, she asked Mr John Attygalle, the then Inspector General of Police, for a transfer to Galle so she could be close to her husband. This was a highly unusual request, since at that time, it was a policy that women police officers should serve only in Colombo and its surrounding suburbs. However, after taking into account her personal circumstances, Mr Attygalle agreed to the transfer and at the end of 1965, Premila became the first female police officer to be stationed outside the Colombo district.

The move to Galle brought other personal happiness as well. Premila's first child, a daughter, was born in 1966. In accordance with the leave policy in that era, Premila took only six weeks of maternity leave. Her mother-in-law and sisters-in-law, with whom she was living, took care of the baby when Premila returned to work. Premila's second daughter was born in 1973, when Premila was back working in Colombo. This time, she was fortunate to have the assistance of her mother and domestic help to look after the baby. Today, Premila is the proud mother of two grown daughters, who are now married and working in their own careers.

Because of the policy that women police officers should serve only in Colombo, Premila had to return to Colombo in 1968. She first worked at Colpetty, then Slave Island, and later in 1971, commenced duty at the Depot Police (later known as the Police Field Force Headquarters). Premila remained at the Depot Police for almost

Premila with her many sports awards

As a senior police officer

23 years, working in administration rather than in field work.

It was at the Depot Police that Premila climbed the ranks of the police force, obtaining several promotions in steady succession. She was promoted to the rank of Sergeant in 1971, about six months after starting there. She then became a Sub-Inspector in 1977, an Inspector in 1984, a Chief Inspector in 1986 and an Assistant Superintendent of Police (ASP) in 1988. Premila eventually rose to the rank of Superintendent of Police (SP) in 1994 and finally, to Senior Superintendent of Police (SSP) in 1999. Premila's promotions were not handed to her on a platter. When she joined the police force in 1959, women could not be promoted beyond the rank of Sergeant. Premila fought for equal promotion rights for women and finally, in the 1970s, women were able to be promoted to the rank of Sub-Inspector and to higher ranks.

In 1994, Premila moved from the Police Field Force Headquarters to head the Children and Women's Bureau, based at the Police Headquarters in Colombo. In this position, in which she reported to the Deputy Inspector General of Police Mr Nizam, Premila worked to help victims of crimes that particularly affect women and children, such as domestic violence and child abuse. Premila notes that such crimes are grossly under-reported, as women and children are reluctant to come forward to the police because of shyness and/or cultural factors. She observes that there are only a handful of shelters where women can escape from violent husbands and these few can only accommodate women for short periods of time. During Premila's tenure from 1994 through 2002, with the help of her colleagues and the Ministry of Women's Affairs, over thirty Children and Women's Desks were established throughout the island. These Desks are staffed by women, to encourage the reporting of crimes.

Ideally, Premila would have established even more Desks across the island, but there were not enough women police officers to staff them. It was thus apparent that the police force could benefit from a greater number of women police officers. Premila would encourage girls and young women to consider a career in the police force, and she especially directs such encouragement to women who have graduated in law. She believes that the police force is an attractive field for women as it provides an opportunity to help people and perform good deeds. Premila has absolutely no regrets about her choice of career. Since her retirement as SSP, there are no senior women in the police force, but Premila has shown that it is possible for women to rise through the ranks. Moreover, it is now possible for women to join the police force at a higher rank (e.g. to directly enter at the Sub-Inspector level) with certain academic qualifications. In Premila's view, it is possible for women to succeed in the police force (and indeed in any chosen profession) with desire, initiative and determination.

The police force also provided Premila with

opportunities to travel overseas. Prior to her position at the Children and Women's Bureau, she travelled abroad for sports meets. Her first meet abroad was in India in 1960 and subsequently, she travelled to a number of international sports meets. As recently as the year 2000, she won the 100m event in her age group at the 11th Asian Veterans athletics championships, held in Bangalore, India. Premila is grateful for the support she has received from the police force in her sporting endeavours. She was given time to train in athletics, as well as in sports that she took up after joining the police force, including basketball and volleyball. In addition, she was able to make use of the facilities at the Police Park in Colombo. Her years at the Children and Women's Bureau also entailed overseas travel. In particular she attended workshops and seminars abroad about twice a year, some of which were organized by Interpol. While these meetings were excellent learning experiences, the police force in Sri Lanka was unfortunately not able to implement all that they learned, due to a lack of resources.

Aside from her posting to Galle from 1965 to 1968, Premila worked outside Colombo only on one other occasion. As a senior police officer, she was required to spend six months in Jaffna from February to August, 1996. This was a dangerous time and her daughters and husband wanted her to retire (which her years of service entitled her to do), instead of going to Jaffna. Premila decided to go and see what the situation was like, but assuaged her family's concerns by agreeing to return if it was too dangerous. When she arrived in Jaffna, she found it was not as hazardous as people had thought, and she successfully completed her six months as head of the police college in Jaffna.

Premila formally retired from the police force in June 1999 at the age of 60. She worked in the police on a contract basis for a further three years from November 1999, finally retiring 'for good' in November 2002. Even in her retirement, however, she has lent her expertise to the Ministry of Women's Affairs (now Ministry of Child Development and Women's Empowerment) in matters of women's and children's security, by giving seminars and talks to schoolchildren, police officers and *grama sevakas* on topics related to child abuse and violence against women.

With her policing days behind her, Premila now enjoys more time with her family, helping to look after her grandchildren in the same way that her mother and mother-in-law once looked after her daughters. One could say now that, through her impressive career as a woman police officer, Premila has led a quiet revolution. As a result of her example, it is clear that women can succeed in unlikely quarters.

Rohini Nanayakkara at the Bank of Ceylon, General Manager's desk

Rohini Nanayakkara
Banker

One can easily see why Rohini, a gracious and elegant lady, has steadily ascended within her profession to become the first woman General Manager and Chief Executive Officer (CEO) of Sri Lanka's largest bank, the Bank of Ceylon (BOC). Effusing natural leadership qualities and revealing her inner confidence, she recounts her past and her achievements with such modesty and poise, that one could only marvel at her calm and quiet determination in giving of her best in whatever she does.

Rohini was born as Rohini Wijeratne on 12 April 1936 in the up-country village of Kotagala, as one of seven children in her family. Her father was a medical practitioner and her mother a housewife. As a doctor in the government service, her father was transferred from town to town, resulting in Rohini attending as many as seven schools! Rohini believes that this somewhat nomadic lifestyle exerted a major impact on her life and greatly shaped her character. She lived in different parts of the country in both rural and urban areas, attending Buddhist, Christian and Catholic girls' schools. Ferguson High School in Ratnapura, St Joseph's Convent in Kegalle and Newstead Girls' College in Negombo were some of the schools that moulded her, prior to her final school years at Methodist College, Colombo where she became a school prefect and acquired the necessary background for a university education.

Rohini recalls that the schools she attended maintained high standards and instilled in her a strong sense of discipline and values. Her varied exposure from being educated in inter-religious and inter-racial environments helped her to accept people for what they are, and to integrate and work with anyone. Interestingly, Rohini does not recall experiencing gender differentiation in working or building relationships. In fact, looking back on her early years in particular, she is at a loss to understand the constant debates on this matter, as her own outlook was based on growing up as part of society in general. When people ask her "Is there a glass ceiling?" or "How did you shatter the glass ceiling?" it sometimes surprises them to hear her view that there is no glass ceiling – if one regards oneself as an equal with men. Clearly, this is one of the greatest hallmarks of Rohini's character, which underpins her climb to the very pinnacle of the corporate ladder with relative ease.

After completing her GCE A-level examination, Rohini had no definite career ambitions. Nor was there pressure from the family for her to pursue a university degree. In fact, her father indicated that he would find it difficult to finance her through university. Yet a natural drive from within her – the desire to do well, to be involved and to be recognized – urged her to pursue her studies. Rohini's door to a university education was opened when her second oldest brother, by then an engineer, said to her parents, "Let her go and I will spend for her education."

Choosing a general Arts degree at the University of Peradeniya, she decided on Economics, History and Philosophy as her subjects. At university, she was a member of the Students' Council and the President of her Hall. When Rohini graduated with second class honours three years later, she was yet undecided about her future. During her era, most women with an Arts degree pursued teaching but Rohini was certain that she would not make a good teacher! Medicine was another popular profession but that was also not an option for her. What should she do? Wisely, Rohini took her time to decide, opting to spend a few months relaxing with her family and waiting for the right opportunity.

Rohini's career interests were aroused when she spotted a newspaper advertisement placed by the BOC, calling for applications for Staff Assistants. The general view at the time was that banks did not hire women graduates. Undeterred, Rohini applied, and was amongst those called for the first interview. She was also selected for the second interview along with 10 to 15 other candidates. The Board of Directors, which was chaired by the well-known lawyer H.V. Perera, interviewed the second round candidates and Rohini was asked many questions. She remembers vividly being asked, "If there is a strike at the bank, would you come to work?" to which she unhesitatingly responded, "Yes, I will."

With these words, Rohini set her feet firmly on her future path. She was selected by the BOC, and on 1 April 1959 commenced employment as the first-ever woman executive at the bank and in the banking sector in Sri Lanka. Along with about a dozen other new entrants, she was based at the BOC's head office in the old Grand Oriental Hotel building in the Fort, and posted to the Personnel Department. Although working in the personnel management area was not exactly what she had in mind, she was committed to the job and performed well.

Rohini spent two years in Personnel. But reminding herself that this was not why she joined the BOC, and fearing that she many never be moved from there, Rohini decided to talk to senior management and made them aware of her banking aspirations. Her efforts were not wasted and before long she was moved to the general banking area. Here she learnt the fundamentals of banking and worked enthusiastically, sometimes staying after hours. Within a few years the BOC had hired more women executives, which implicitly demonstrated that Rohini had proved herself as a capable female executive. By the mid-1960s, Rohini had risen to the grade of Manager and was attached to the Credit and Loans Department. Her eight or so years in this department was a wonderful opportunity from which she gained valuable insights into the nucleus of banking – relationship and credit management.

During the early 1970s, the Government was undertaking macro-economic reforms in the country's plantation sector, and Rohini was offered a role on a special project in the tea industry's Agency House reforms. She was enthused by the offer as it presented an opportunity for a temporary break from banking. Besides, changing jobs was not an issue, as the BOC would second her to this role. Not long after she decided to accept the offer and started on her new project, she was sent to London to study the tea auction system. This certainly was a move destined for her, since it was in London that she met Cyril Nanayakkara who was attached to the Sri Lankan High Commission. He was to be her husband and

Rohini at her graduation, 1959

future partner!

Notwithstanding the joys of their romance, Rohini dutifully returned to Sri Lanka upon completion of her work in London, but her return home was not to be for long, since Cyril and Rohini decided to marry in 1971 and move back to London. This time, she was able to take long leave from the BOC. London is where Rohini was first exposed to working in a foreign banking environment upon joining one of the United Kingdom's premier financial institutions, the Midland Bank. It was also in London that their first child, a son, was born. Thus the time Rohini spent in London turned out to be a very special period in her life.

After living in London for a year and a half, Rohini and Cyril returned to Sri Lanka and Rohini moved back to the BOC, this time as Branch Manager of the Wellawatte branch. Once again, she broke new ground as the first woman to manage a BOC branch. She found that shouldering responsibilities and taking decisions were right up her alley and she enjoyed the role tremendously. Soon after, their second son was born. Yet Rohini continued to work, being fortunate to receive great support from her parents.

Rohini's life was a sea of change! In the late 1970s, Cyril was appointed to a posting in Brussels. And so it was time to pack their bags once again. There is no doubt that Rohini was an enormously talented individual who possessed the ability to quickly adjust herself; not only to balance family life and a challenging career, but also to move and settle in different environments with relative ease. Availing herself of a provision to take no-pay leave from the BOC, Rohini joined her husband in Brussels. An opportunist by nature, Rohini found this an ideal time to study French, and after completion of a diploma in the language, joined the Bank Bruxelles Lambert where she was able to further develop in the all-important area of relationship banking and notably, in an international banking environment.

After three and a half years, the family returned to Sri Lanka. During the period Rohini was in Belgium (which lasted until the early 1980s), Sri Lanka experienced a period of significant change under a newly elected Government. Licensed foreign banks were permitted to operate under the Government's open economy initiatives and, consequently, some of the largest international financial institutions such as American Express, Citibank and Deutsche Bank established operations in Sri Lanka. It seemed an apt time for her return, as in recognition of her valuable international exposure, Rohini was promoted yet again – this time to Senior Manager.

Naturally, it was a challenging time for BOC and it had to step up to meet the new competition. Fortunately, the bank had a progressive outlook. The bank's dynamic Chairman at the time, Nissanka Wijewardena, decided to pursue a restructuring program in consultation with the International Finance Corporation in Washington DC and based on her proven capabilities and overseas experience, Rohini was offered the role of coordinating the restructuring team. Working with high-profile consultants from the USA and India for nearly three years, she received tremendous exposure to the specialised area of restructuring.

To remain competitive, BOC embarked upon several major projects, which included the launch in 1981 of a new head office building. This attracted great interest, as it would be Sri Lanka's first high-rise building. Once again, Rohini was BOC's choice to act as coordinator for the building project. Aware of the importance of acquiring broad management skills to reach the higher echelons of corporations, Rohini accepted the role. "To get to the top, one needs both banking and management," she says. This new role steered her towards yet another new experience. She had to deal closely with architects, consultants, engineers, lawyers and a myriad of other specialist service providers in order to successfully complete the project. It was a huge logistical task to move hundreds of staff to the new building, but not surprisingly, Rohini stepped up to this challenge. In 1987, the imposing tower in the Fort was completed, and amidst a grand ceremony, the new headquarters opened its doors

Fittingly, she received yet another promotion. This time she made the grade of Assistant General Manager, once again becoming the first woman to reach this position at BOC. Being a state bank, there were lengthy procedures to be followed when it came to promotions, unlike in the private sector. However in this instance, it seemed possible for the Board to decide relatively quickly on Rohini's promotion based on her highly visible and outstanding performance. In her new position, Rohini headed the newly founded Corporate Branch in the plush new offices, set in luxurious surroundings with modern facilities and technology.

During this period the American government invited Rohini for a fully funded one month visit to the United States, under the auspices of the International Visitor Program. Persons were invited under this program on the basis of their strong leadership potential. Rohini was greeted in Washington DC where a program was devised to suit her requirements, taking into account, her professional aspirations as well as tourist interests. She met with various high-

Launch of children's mobile savings bank, Ferguson High School, Ratnapura, June 1990

ranking officials at major banks across the US, learning about new products and systems, whilst also being shown famous tourist attractions such as the Niagara Falls and the Grand Canyon. She was accommodated with local families, adding an interesting dimension to the tour. This trip is one of the highlights of her illustrious career, and memories of this unique opportunity evoke in her, a great sense of honour and joy.

When she returned from her tour of the US, Rohini learned that the BOC's General Manager and CEO was due to retire. Undoubtedly, Rohini, with her broad experience and management capabilities, was eligible for promotion and was a key candidate for the post. This was the only time Rohini recalls a promotion becoming an issue for her, for the question on everyone's mind was "Can a woman lead the bank?" Being such a high-profile position, the financial market was also abuzz with rumours and the same issue was being discussed within the financial community. During this crucial time of her career she recollects banking being regarded by many as a "man's world." It was considered disadvantageous to employ women because they could not work late and could not be sent on out-of-office assignments. This was a perception issue, which necessitated women having to prove themselves at every turn. Although there had earlier been times she and other women had to speak out in order to be recognized, gender was never an issue, as it seemed to have become with regards to the highly visible GM position.

In her forthright manner, Rohini decided to speak to the Chairman, Dr Nimal Sandaratne on this matter. Quite appropriately, she simply said to Dr Sandaratne "I hope that gender would not be a deciding factor." The Chairman assured her of an unbiased assessment. She was called up for a near three-hour interview with the Board and questioned on all aspects of banking and management. Her articulate responses and ability to talk freely and candidly about the bank's operations, her performance and specialised experience, certainly impressed them and she was appointed GM, thus capping a remarkable and admirable career.

Rohini was to commence her new position on 10 November 1988. She never anticipated her appointment would coincide with a tumultuous period in the country's history. It was the time of the "JVP insurrection" and the day she was to assume duties, the JVP had planned a *hartal*. The whole country came to a standstill with shops and offices closed, and, amidst this chaos, she was expected to take charge of the country's largest bank! Remaining true to her pledge at her final interview with BOC decades ago where she had responded she would come to work despite a strike, she decided to start work on the appointed day, thereby honouring the trust and confidence

Rohini Nanayakkara as General Manager, Bank of Ceylon

placed in her when the Board of Directors had decided to hire her in 1959.

With no BOC chauffeurs reporting for duty that day, it was up to her husband Cyril, to drive her to work through a virtual ghost city. A handful of staff who were aware that she was turning up for work also braved their way to the 29th floor of their headquarters. Following a small ceremony arranged in her honour, Rohini soon settled down to the tasks ahead, even succeeding in opening the BOC doors for business that day! The difficult process of opening and closing the bank periodically during these uncertain times continued for nearly six months. It was a dangerous period, particularly when staff were threatened if they went to work, sometimes with death. Through all these dangers and upheavals, Rohini continued, with a calm and composed approach, taking everything in her stride.

She remained as GM and CEO for seven years, before retiring in 1996 after an illustrious career with the BOC. Firmly believing in kindness, generosity, fair play, and equal opportunity, Rohini demonstrated a natural flair for fostering inter personal relationships and problem solving, consistently motivated by the best interests of the bank and its employees. A touching farewell tribute titled 'Farewell, Fair Lady' presented by the Bank of Ceylon branch of the Ceylon Bank Employees Union fondly expressed deep appreciation of her personal qualities, which were the ingredients of Rohini's remarkably successful banking career.

Retirement from the BOC was not the end of her career, nor the end of her services to the country's financial development. She assumed a two-year position with the Ministry of Finance in a World Bank project to set up a private sector infrastructure development fund. Yearning to return to the world of banking, Rohini joined Seylan Bank as its CEO in October 1998, becoming the first woman CEO of a private sector bank. She also served as a Director of Seylan and several other Ceylinco Group companies. After a challenging five year period with the Ceylinco Group, Rohini decided to step down and plan her future in semi-retirement. Currently, she is Chairman of the Board of Directors of the financial services group, Lanka Orix, and is on the boards of many other companies, thus continuing to draw on her in-depth business experience and help others to succeed.

Confirming her status as one of the nation's leading and most respected managers, Rohini was appointed by H.E. the President to the Task Force to Rebuild the Nation (TAFREN) following the devastating tsunami that tragically impacted the country in December 2004. Later converted to a Statutory Board, Rohini remains on the Board as a Director working with the several donors that offered assistance towards the massive rebuilding program.

Rohini has gained immense satisfaction from her banking career. "One should be happy joining a bank," she says. "It is a great experience and a great service. To advise others and to see them prosper is wonderful." She has travelled to many parts of the world and met with leading bankers in Europe, Asia and the US, gaining invaluable knowledge that she was able to impart to the BOC. She has been hosted in plush boardrooms around the world, many a time being told how graceful she looks in the saree (which was always her official attire).

Rohini had no role model per se. She was in effect, her own driving force, wanting to do well at all times. However, she gained much from her superiors, recalling the high standards and values set by the GMs in her time, and the very professional top echelons of management. She was therefore able to model herself on those lines and be fair, objective, and non-discriminatory. Her advice to aspiring CEOs is the following: "When you are CEO, it is very important to recognise people for their talents and give them opportunities. The key to building a successful team is to provide learning opportunities here and overseas."

Her message to women is that "they should not feel inferior in any way – after all, men and women are given equal opportunity in education, so why feel inferior? When opportunities come your way, one must establish credibility. Women have the ability to perform better than men do, as they are good at applying themselves. Be assertive when required and speak up for your advancement and promotions."

One of the greatest qualities in Rohini is her ability to get on with the job. Looking back on her days as CEO at the BOC where she was required to take some of the toughest decisions in her life, she did not think of it as bravery or courage. To her, it was a matter of duty, and duty came first. Moreover, her husband's full support was with her all the way and he did not interfere in her decisions. In fact it was her younger son who summed it up very appropriately when he said to her one day, "Amma, you are a person who does not dwell too much on the pros and cons. If you wanted to do something you did it." She had to agree that her son's words made her aware of a deeply rooted truth about herself!

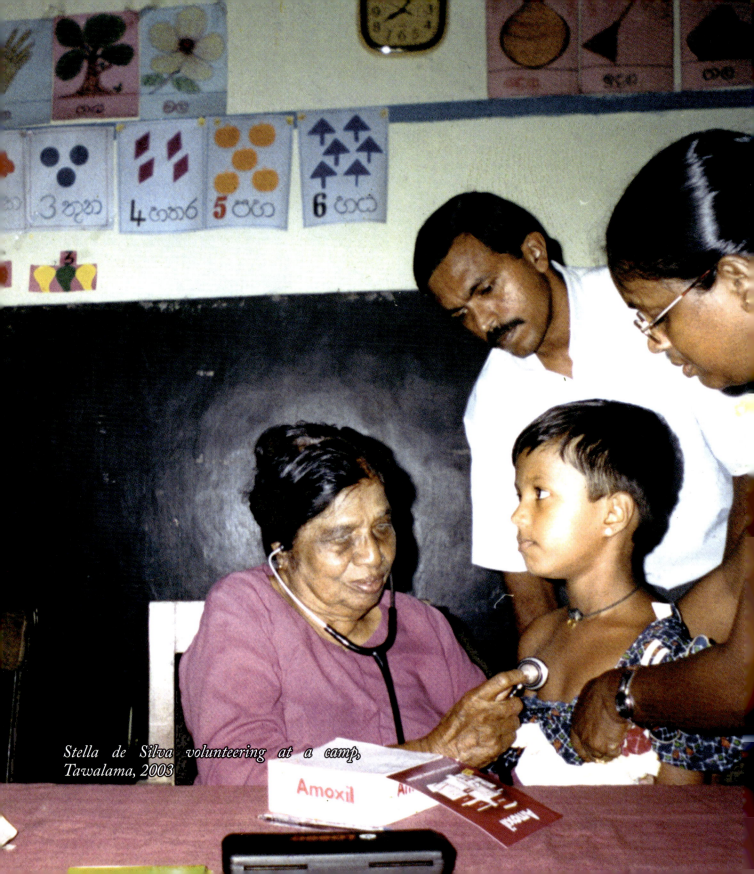
Stella de Silva volunteering at a camp, Tawalama, 2003

Dr Stella de Silva
Paediatrician

Sri Lanka is fortunate to have been gifted with a medical specialist of the calibre of Dr Stella de Silva. After graduating from the University of Ceylon with First Class Honours and a distinction in surgery in 1942, "Dr Stella" (as she is affectionately known) became one of the country's most sought after paediatricians. For well over half a century, she treated countless young patients, imparted her knowledge to successive cohorts of medical students, and helped to improve the general health and well-being of the poor in rural communities. Stella's outstanding commitment and contributions to medical services in the nation have left a lasting improvement in the lives of many Sri Lankans.

Born on 2 June 1918 in Randombe, Balapitiya, in southern Sri Lanka, Stella had a very happy and simple childhood. In her early years, she attended a local school, Prajapathy Vidyalaya, in Ambalangoda. She remembers the joy of going to school in a bullock cart, and returning home to play with her siblings and several cousins who lived nearby. Her father, C.R. de Silva, was a well known lawyer who practised at the Balapitiya law courts. Her mother Adeline was a busy housewife, who ably shouldered the responsibility of raising six children, four boys and two girls. Stella was their fourth child and the younger of two daughters.

When she reached the age of 7, Stella's parents sent her and her elder sister Gladys to the hostel of Southlands College, Galle, a leading girls' school in the region. Growing up, Stella remembers being an untidy girl who frequently managed to spoil her pristine white school uniforms with splashes of ink. She recalls with laughter how her sister was in the habit of borrowing Stella's petticoats. Of course, sharing garments was not uncommon amongst sisters. But Stella had to deal with an awkward situation; she was much leaner than her sister Gladys who found an innovative way of fitting into them – she slit Stella's petticoats and expanded the garments so she could wear them. Obviously, the petticoats were not much use to Stella thereafter!

Stella acquired a great love for books at a young age, her favourite genre being murder mystery and in particular, the works of Agatha Christie. She attributes her enduring passion for reading to Miss Edith Ridge, a Scottish lady who travelled to Sri Lanka to become Vice Principal of Southlands College a few years after

Stella joined the school and who later became Principal in 1935, when she took over the reins of the school from Miss Mabel Freethy.

Ever since she can remember, Stella wanted to study medicine. "I always wanted to do medicine – even as a young girl," she said. In those days it was virtually unheard of for girls to pursue a medical career but that did not in any way diminish her aspirations.

Stella's father, however, had different ideas. Aware that medicine was an expensive course of study, and conscious of his responsibilities to educate all six of his children, he favoured a teaching career for his younger daughter. Fortunately, however, Stella had the support of her oldest brother Percy, whom she most admired in the family and who had always been a great inspiration. He willingly offered to fund her education to enable her to follow her heart. Percy was a civil servant, but was later better known as "C.P." the politician, and as a minister in the cabinet of S.W.R.D. Bandaranaike, Sri Lanka's Prime Minister from 1956 to 1959.

To realise her dream of becoming a doctor, she had to overcome another hurdle; the lack of science facilities at Southlands College. While this was clearly an enormous impediment to Stella's professional ambitions, it did not dampen the spirits of this determined young woman. She soon learnt that it was possible for her to study the required science subjects at Richmond College, a neighbouring boys' school. Somewhat surprisingly, this unusual educational arrangement was encouraged by both Miss Freethy and Miss Ridge and indeed, the latter even offered to provide transport to and from Richmond College, most likely because she believed a young girl should not be sent un-chaperoned to a boys' school! Buoyed by the support of the head staff at Southlands, Stella quickly seized this rare opportunity to further her scientific studies.

Stella was a high achiever throughout her school career, and not just as a scholar. She became Head Girl of Southlands, was a girl guide, and engaged in several sports including netball, tennis and horse-riding. Academically, she was a shining star. She passed the Junior Cambridge and later the Senior Cambridge Examinations with top honours to gain admission to the Ceylon Medical College at the age of 17. Moreover, she won a scholarship, and hence the issue of funding her tertiary education did not arise. She was also exempted from the one-year pre-medical course that was included in the six-year medical degree, highlighting a stunning performance.

Embarking on a medical degree in 1937 required her to move from the familiar comforts of her rather rural lifestyle to the more urban

Stella meeting Prince Charles, circa 1982

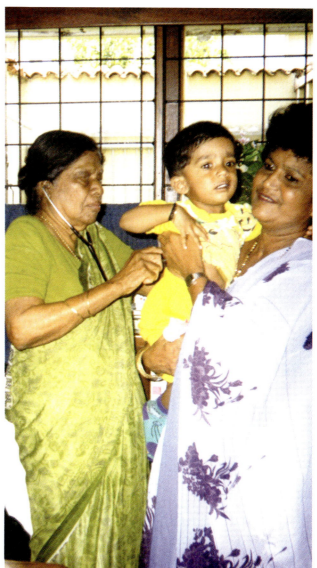

Stella with a young patient

surroundings of Colombo. Her experience away from her family began at the Cruden Hostel for University Women at Queen's Road and in the final year she moved to a private house in Barnes Place, Cinnamon Gardens, which was owned by the family of Dr Nora Walpola (née Joseph).

Her brother Arthur (informally known as "A.H."), who studied mathematics and then law, together with Leslie (informally known as "L.B."), who studied chemistry, obtained a PhD and worked at the Medical Research Institute, were residing nearby at Brodie House, a university hostel for men. They, together with Merryl, another of her brothers, were Stella's most frequent visitors. Like two of his brothers C.P. and A.H., Merryl would later enter politics but he was also a recognised sportsman, having represented Sri Lanka internationally in boxing. Stella looked forward to these many fraternal visits, though she was inclined to believe her brothers' primary motivation was to meet the other resident female students!

It was during her days at Medical College that Stella formed some of her closest friendships. Buddhimati Jayasundera, Beatrice Dharmaratne, Kamala Carthigesu, Doreen Jayawardene, Leela Candiah, and Muriel Dharmaratne were amongst her dearest friends. Buddhimati was blessed with the luxury of living with her parents in Colombo and Stella fondly recollects Buddhimati's regular visits, armed with delicious home-cooked food. A treasured treat that was often included among the delectable fare was the traditional breakfast comprising string hoppers and *pol sambol*. Doreen, still alive, as is Muriel, frequently visits Stella even now.

Stella graduated in 1942, realising her childhood dream of becoming a doctor. Following a year's work as a House Officer in the Galle and Avissawella hospitals, she embarked on a seven year period of clinical training attached to the Teaching Hospitals, University of Ceylon, Colombo in 1944. During this period she held several positions, beginning as Resident House Physician to Dr L.O. Abeyratne, Consultant Paediatrician at the Lady Ridgeway Hospital for Children and concluding as a Medical Registrar in Internal Medicine at the General Hospital, Colombo. In between these two positions, she also served as Resident House Surgeon, Resident House Physician and Senior House Physician under eminent consultants and professors in fields as diverse as obstetrics and gynaecology, eye surgery, and anaesthesiology.

During those quite exhaustive years of training and employment, Stella had the privilege of working with some of the country's most brilliant specialists, thereby enabling her to develop a valuable range of skills. She was particularly inspired by Dr L.O. Abeyratne, the country's first trained specialist paediatrician who was appointed in 1937 as physician and medical officer in charge at the Lady Ridgeway Hospital in Colombo. Indeed, it was during her training period with this distinguished doctor that Stella became conscious of her propensity for treating children.

The opportunity to specialise in paediatrics arose in 1952, when the Sri Lankan Government, recognising Stella's outstanding ability and talent, awarded her a two-year scholarship for postgraduate training in the UK. She trained in London for a year at the renowned Institute of Child Health, which is attached to the Great Ormond Street Hospital for Children. There, she was part of an internationally diverse student body which included trainees from North and South Rhodesia, South Africa, Australia, New Zealand, India, Indonesia, Burma and Syria. Incorporated in her program was a year at the Royal Post-Graduate Medical School, Hammersmith Hospital, a large and well-known teaching hospital in the city of London.

While in the UK, Stella cruised through the requisite examinations to obtain the internationally known qualifications of DCH (Diploma in Child Health) in 1953, MRCP (London) in 1954 and MRCP (Edinburgh) in the same year. It is believed that she was the first woman from South East Asia to obtain the "double" MRCP qualification, succeeding in both examinations at the first attempt. It was a challenging period during which she had to combine clinical work with studies and examinations. Despite her hectic schedule however, Stella found time to enjoy the London theatre scene and to travel – some of her favoured recreational pastimes.

Stella stepped into her long and illustrious career in paediatrics when in November 1954, she returned to her homeland and was immediately appointed as Registrar, Resident Paediatrician OPD (Out Patients Department) and Physician at Lady Ridgeway Hospital. Not long afterwards, in 1956, she obtained the qualification of Doctor of Medicine (MD) (Ceylon), and is understood to be the first Sri Lankan woman to be conferred this degree.

With the appointment in 1959 as Consultant Paediatrician at Lady Ridgeway, as well as at Castle Street Hospital and De Soysa Maternity Hospital, Stella greatly expanded the scope of her work. She taught undergraduate and postgraduate medical students, and nurses and midwives, in addition to treating children in all three hospitals – her career straddling the fields of medicine and academia. Having on several occasions stood in for the then Professor of Paediatrics, Dr C.C. de Silva when called upon to assist in the university's teaching programmes,

Stella with her postgraduate training class in the UK, 1952

Stella's farewell at the Lady Ridgeway Hospital, 1973

Stella seemed the obvious choice to succeed him as Professor of Paediatrics, Faculty of Medicine at the University of Ceylon. However, on being offered the post in 1965, she chose to decline this prestigious appointment citing the depth of her professional commitments at the time.

Animated by advancements in the medical field, she decided to gain further expertise and specialisation overseas. In 1967, she accepted a year-long Fulbright Scholarship to work as a Research Fellow in New York at the renowned Babies Hospital, which formed part of Columbia-Presbyterian Medical Center. Stella immensely enjoyed her sojourn in New York, valuing in particular the exposure she received to sophisticated medical facilities and systems which greatly simplified her work.

Stella returned to Sri Lanka the following year and resumed her role at Lady Ridgeway Hospital, and, in 1973, was promoted to Senior Paediatrician and Consultant. Stella, who by then was awarded fellowships (FRCP) from Edinburgh as well as from London, retired from government service later in the year at the age of 55, after more than three decades of dedicated service to the general public.

In recognition of her outstanding contribution to Sri Lanka's premier children's hospital, her portrait was unveiled at a farewell ceremony by Dr L.O. Abeyratne, who glowingly described her as "his best pupil ever"; high praise indeed but an assessment surely shared by many of her mentors.

Despite her retirement from Lady Ridgeway, Stella was certainly not ready to "hang up her stethoscope". She turned her energy solely towards treating children privately from her home. In 1985, at the age of 67, she was offered the position of Professor and Head of the Department of Paediatrics at North Colombo Medical College (NCMC), Sri Lanka's first private medical school founded in association with the Colombo North General Hospital in Ragama. She accepted the position without hesitation. Here she trained and inspired both undergraduate and postgraduate medical students for ten years, underscoring her deep-rooted interest in academia. It was only in 1995, at the eminent age of 77 years, that Stella formally concluded an exceptionally long and distinguished career as one of the most prominent doctors in Sri Lanka.

Throughout her tenure at public hospitals and at NCMC, she also treated children on a private basis, initially, at a residence in Dharmapala Mawatha which she shared with two of her brothers, C.P. and L.B., in the early days of her career. After building and moving into her own house in Horton Place, she continued to treat children there, as well as at Dr Lilly Arumugam's consultation rooms at Alexandra Place. Stella's ability to successfully combine public and private practice over several decades is a testament to the depth of her dedication and commitment to her patients, which frequently entailed long and arduous working hours.

Stella's multi-faceted contributions to the medical field have been aptly recognised by several associations and organisations. Admitted as a Fellow of the Sri Lanka College of Paediatricians in 1997, she was conferred many honorary positions during her career, including President of the Sri Lanka Paediatric Association (which in 1996, became the Sri Lanka College of Paediatricians) in 1980/81. She was also President of the Sri Lanka Medical Association in the year 1981/82 during which she represented Sri Lanka at the 150th anniversary celebrations of the British Medical Association in the UK. She recalls being dressed for that special occasion in a classic cashmere silk saree, and was honoured to have received a memento from Charles, Prince of Wales.

Throughout her career, she was closely associated with the Sri Lanka Medical Library – not only as a past President of the library, but also as an author of several articles published in the Ceylon Medical Journal, the quarterly journal of the Sri Lanka Medical Association. Additionally, Stella was the Editor/Editor Emeritus of the Sri Lanka Journal of Child Health (Ceylon Journal of Child Health prior to 2000) – the official publication of the Sri Lanka College of Paediatricians – from 1967 to 2003, a record 36 years! Her wealth of experience was also recognised well beyond Sri Lankan shores. She enthusiastically accepted invitations to deliver medical papers at several conferences overseas, including at the International Congress of Paediatrics in Montreal, Lisbon, and Buenos Aires.

In 1994, the Sri Lanka Government bestowed upon Stella the national honour of *Vidya Jyothi* for her outstanding contributions to science and medicine. Following her receipt of this prestigious award, Stella paid tribute to her former principal and mentor, the much loved Miss Ridge. "You taught me humility and the joy of healing" and "to knit together in love and service," she said of her. Indeed it was her early association with Miss Ridge that defined her life and steered her towards the study of medicine. Her several visits to the UK as an adult, would not have been complete without a visit to Scotland to see her inspirational first mentor; a clear indication of the affection and deep gratitude for a fine lady who exerted such a positive influence on her young life.

A very socially conscious individual, Stella has long extended her knowledge and services to less privileged communities in the South of Sri Lanka – the region of her youth – as well as in the North Central province. She has conducted clinics and addressed seminars primarily in nutrition and family planning. During the years she was attached to the NCMC, she volunteered her services to treat children at the Children's Convalescent Home at Ragama that accommodated approximately thirty children. She served on the Board of Trustees in 1999 and was actively involved in various ways until 2006. When the devastating tsunami struck in December 2004, Stella rallied yet again. Gathering a team of specialists and undeterred by her age of 86 years at the time, she travelled to Galle – one of the worst affected towns – to distribute medicines and treat scores of people who required urgent medical attention.

Fortunate to have eluded any major setbacks during her medical career, when asked about the obstacles she faced, she recalls only the challenges of being a fresh graduate during the Second World War. One Sunday evening, soon after she qualified, she was enjoying a movie with some friends at the Majestic Cinema in Bambalapitya when the cinema hall suddenly erupted in a blast of sirens and there was a panicked evacuation of the moviegoers. It was only later that she learnt about the Japanese air raid on Colombo harbour. While the country faced a scarcity of food during the war, she steadfastly carried on with the rigours of hospital ward rounds and attending to patients while snacking on peanuts and other small consumables.

Nor did she face any gender-based discrimination as one of the country's leading female specialists. "If you were good, you were accepted," she explains simply. That is not to say, however, that she was shielded from the normal day-to-day challenges that arose regularly throughout her career. In particular, the emotional stress of treating gravely ill children who required round-the-clock attention was a constantly taxing aspect of her work.

Driven by a rare passion for healing and service, and believing that she would not be able to impart her best to patients unless she adopted a rigorous work ethic and remained completely dedicated to her work, Stella deliberately chose a demanding medical career over marriage. In fact, her life revolved so much around medicine that her brothers used to tease her about her ignorance of all matters other than medicine!

Not true, for, in reality Stella did find and enjoy life outside the sphere of medicine. She is a founding member of the Zonta Club of Colombo, which forms part of Zonta International, an organisation dedicated to advancing the status of women worldwide. She has travelled to Germany, the USA and Australia to attend conferences in furtherance of Zonta's mission. In 1983, for example, she pioneered the Zonta Service Project to provide clean drinking water for thousands of settlers in the Mahaweli development area of Kalawewa, in Sri Lanka's dry zone.

Beyond her civic activities, the theatre was a favourite pastime of Stella's. Whenever she could carve out a few hours from a hectic schedule that required her to treat patients, deliver a lecture, chair a meeting, and write an article – not unusual in a day's work – she would make her way to the Lionel Wendt theatre to be entertained by the plays and other performances staged there. She was also a competent seamstress, often choosing to stitch her own saree jackets. Above all, Stella is grateful for the company of books, particularly as the years have passed and her physical health has declined.

Now having celebrated her ninetieth birthday after a lifetime of passionately devoted service to the medical profession, she continues to live contentedly at her home on Horton Place. She is rarely alone; family and friends – amongst them Doreen, her long-standing ally from Medical School days – are regular companions, and she has always had live-in domestic help, ensuring the smooth functioning of the household. Two of her nieces, Kanthi and Anoma, are especially close to Stella and have provided her with increasing support and security in recent years.

Stella is a great source of inspiration to all her nieces and nephews, as well as to their children. Medicine was always an interesting and much discussed subject among the younger members of the family. But she wisely instructed them: "Never do medicine because of me," and emphasised that one should not study medicine without a genuine desire and love for it. Her advice to young doctors is simple and astute: "Broaden your outlook and experience by going out into the world and seeing for yourselves the advances in medical science. Use what you have learnt and seen abroad and serve your country." What wise counsel, spoken by one of the truly outstanding doctors in Sri Lanka, and one who has practised exactly that!

Sumitra Peries shooting Sagara Galaya, 1987

Sumitra Peries
Film Director

Throughout the cinematic world, female directors are a rare breed, and in this respect, Sri Lanka is no exception. Yet Sumitra Peries boldly entered into film directing in her youth, and since then, has shone spectacularly in it. Sumitra's creative success is a testament to her amazing spirit, which exudes a sense of freedom, adventure and imaginative expression.

Sumitra Peries' life began and first unfolded in a fairly conventional way. She was born Sumitra Gunawardena in the village of Paiyagala, and had her early education in the town of Avissawella, where her father, Harry Gunawardena, had a successful practice as a proctor. Although Sumitra's father came from a political family famously associated with the Left – his brother was the well-known activist, Philip Gunawardena – and once contested a seat in the State Council, he did not pursue a career in politics. Sumitra's mother, Harriette (née Wickramasinghe), was a strong maternal figure in the Gunawardena household. By contrast with the progressive and sometimes radical influences of Sumitra's paternal relatives, Harriette Gunawardena ensured that her children had a traditional and rather strict upbringing. Sumitra was the third-born child in the family, being preceded by her elder brother Gamini and older sister Chandralatha, while the youngest in the family was her brother Ranjith. Growing up, Sumitra was especially close to her brother Gamini, who would later become a mentor and great supporter of her creative interests.

The young Sumitra schooled at St Mary's College in Avissawella until the age of about 9, whereupon she left to join her sister in the hostel of Visakha Vidyalaya in Colombo. Sumitra attended Visakha in the post-war years, from 1945 to 1951. She recalls that Visakha was then a traditional girls' school, which did not nurture its students' interest in artistic and creative fields. The cleverer girls tended to follow the science stream at school and several of them each year would end up as doctors, while students in the arts stream generally did not pursue their own careers.

Sumitra's interest in the theatre and cinema was fostered by her brother Gamini (familiarly known as 'Kuru'), who had a great love of literature and the arts. While a law student at university, he would take his young sister along to plays starring such actors as Iranganie

Serasinghe, and to see classic films from abroad at the major cinemas. However, it would be a while before Sumitra contemplated a foray into filmmaking herself, since an artistic cinematic industry had not yet developed in Sri Lanka at the time. This was the era of Rukmani Devi and B.A.W. Jayamanne, when Sinhala films were much more commercial than creative. In fact, schoolgirls were often discouraged from even watching local films, which were frowned upon as 'entertainment for the masses'!

In 1949, Sumitra's mother moved to Colombo to a house situated just near Visakha, mainly so that Sumitra and her sisters could move out of the hostel. Sumitra lived there with her siblings as well as four of her cousins who were also schooling in Colombo. Unfortunately, however, this familial togetherness was to be short-lived. Sumitra's mother died a year after moving to Colombo, when Sumitra was only fourteen years old.

In many ways, the untimely death of her mother marked a seminal moment in Sumitra's life. Her sister stopped going to school to help look after Sumitra and their other siblings and cousins. Sumitra was able to return to her secondary education, this time at Aquinas College, at the age of 17 to study for the London A-levels. Yet despite this personal cataclysm, Sumitra came to enjoy greater freedom; she was no longer restrained by the rules and traditions which her mother had upheld and thereafter could lead a fairly liberal life. Sumitra is cognisant that she may not have been able to make the same choices in life had her mother not passed away.

Sumitra's brother Gamini, devastated by the loss of his mother, disappeared from Sri Lanka to travel overseas. Most of his mother's property had been left to him, in the hope that he – as the eldest child – would oversee and multiply it. But Gamini was a cerebral human being who was not interested in money and money-making, and he donated everything he had before leaving Sri Lanka. Sumitra remembers this as a very symbolic act at a formative time, which set a humane and selfless example for the rest of the family to follow. As a result, observes Sumitra, none of her siblings fought over money and possessions like in many other families. Instead of accumulating wealth, they acquired knowledge and the feeling that life is more meaningful with greater contact with people than money.

After leaving Aquinas, Sumitra hoped to go abroad and so she contacted Gamini, who was by then living on a yacht off the south of France with a French painter friend and his wife. Buoyed by a sense of adventure and wanderlust rare in young women of her time, Sumitra boldly proceeded on a ship alone to Europe in 1956, to join her brother on the Mediterranean. Though she had never been abroad, she recalls nonchalantly telling her father that she was leaving Sri Lanka and that her brother would come to meet her when her ship reached Naples. Being a relaxed and liberal-minded father, Harry Gunawardena admirably did not dissuade his daughter from going.

Sumitra lived on the yacht with her brother for several months, spending much of her time in the famous town of Saint-Tropez on the French Riviera. It was an eye-opening experience for a girl of twenty, being exposed to a bohemian lifestyle and liberal social scene which she would not have encountered in Sri Lanka. There was partying, night-clubbing and drinking aplenty, but with the in-built checks of a traditional Sri Lankan upbringing, Sumitra was not swept up by these diversions. She knew she wanted something more satisfying in life and while absorbing the many new vistas around her, she contemplated her future.

After a few months on the yacht, Sumitra had had enough and asked herself: "Where I am going?" She was sure she wanted to pursue a path in the arts rather than the sciences, and was interested in psychology or architecture. Though her brother was keen to be a writer, this was not something that attracted Sumitra. She felt that she didn't have the skills to be a writer and being so interested in people, would have found it too solitary an activity. Sumitra had long loved the movies and began to consider being involved in filmmaking. In Saint-Tropez, Sumitra had seen Brigitte Bardot during the making of the legendary French film *Et Dieu… créa la femme* (And God Created Woman). She pondered the possibility of using a camera to record what was happening around her, as a documentary, and discussed this idea with her brother. Eventually, on Gamini's advice, she decided to go to Switzerland to learn French, enrolling herself at the well-known Ecole de français moderne (now the Ecole de français langue étrangère) at the University of Lausanne. Sumitra's mother had left her some inheritance, which she sold to use for her studies. After dropping his younger sister off in Lausanne, Gamini headed back to Sri Lanka.

By the end of her time in Lausanne, Sumitra knew she wanted to enter into filmmaking; she was just undecided as to whether she wished to do feature films. In 1957, after a year in Lausanne, Sumitra travelled to Paris. There was a very good film school there – the IDEC – where she was determined to go. Dishearteningly, however, she was told she needed an extra year of French to enroll there. Fortunately, it so happened that Sumitra met Lester James Peries in Paris around this time; he had come to France to show his film

Sumitra as a bridesmaid at a friend's wedding, 1953

Rekawa (The Line) at the Cannes Film Festival. In fact, Sumitra saw *Rekawa* for the first time in Paris, at a showing organised by the Sri Lankan embassy there. Lester counselled Sumitra to go to London, where there was a very good film school called the London School of Film Technique. Because of the prevailing anti-colonial sentiment in Sri Lanka (that she personally shared), Sumitra had earlier not considered studying in London. On Lester's advice, however, she went there in 1957 and graduated two years later with a Diploma in Film Direction and Production.

For a short while after her studies, Sumitra worked in London as a subtitler at the eponymous firm of the well-known editor Mai Harris. But Sumitra was not enamoured with continuing to work in London. She found subtitling quite dull, and life in London to be rather humdrum compared with her colourful time in Europe. Late in 1959, her brother Gamini wrote to her from Sri Lanka with an interesting proposal. He told her that Lester was directing another film – *Sandesaya* (The Message) – and asked whether she would want to come back and work with him. Keen to put into practice all she had learned at film school, Sumitra decided to seize this opportunity and return to Sri Lanka.

Sumitra worked with Lester as an assistant director on *Sandesaya*, and in 1963, as an assistant director and editor on his next film, *Gamperaliya*

(Changes in the Village). These were tremendous learning experiences, which set the stage for her editing several more award-winning films and eventually, directing her own films. Sumitra explains that back then, working on sets took much longer. Filmmakers needed to wait for the right light, the sun, the rain and so forth, and spending six months on location was not unusual. But as always, Sumitra adapted easily to different surroundings. Even as a young girl, she recalls that when they went to visit relatives who would then ask the kids to stay, she was always the first one to say "Yes!", a trait which would provoke stern stares from her mother!

Just before the making of *Gamperaliya*, Lester, Sumitra and Anton Wickramasinghe (a friend of Lester's) formed a film company called Cinelanka Ltd. Sumitra put her own money into the company, thereby becoming an investor in *Gamperaliya*. Sumitra felt that her financial investment in the film enabled her to be considered a serious player in the industry; and in particular, the right to edit *Gamperaliya*.

In 1964, Lester and Sumitra were married, sealing a deep emotional and creative bond which had developed during their collaborative work. Though Sumitra entered the world of filmmaking on her own accord, Lester has guided and encouraged her throughout her professional endeavours, giving her the space to grow both as a person and as a filmmaker. In 1969, Sumitra won a scholarship to study in France for a year, at the Conservatoire Indépendent du Cinéma Français. Lester was entirely supportive of Sumitra being away for this extended period of time and Sumitra returned to Sri Lanka after a year and a half away.

This extended time in France cemented the already influential impact of French culture on Sumitra's work. Sumitra has read widely in French, including existentialist writers such as Sartre as well as other French authors. She holds in high esteem French film directors like Robert Bresson, Jean-Luc Goddard, François Truffaut and Louis Malle. It is evident that Sumitra's work has been influenced by the subtle and refined visual quality of French films, which she far prefers to their harsher American counterparts. Sumitra observes that French cinema is much more a medium of expression than a commercial product and indeed, this attribute is also apparent in Sumitra's own work. It is thus unsurprising that she bcmoans the increasing hold of Bollywood over Sri Lankan audiences, given the direction which the Indian film industry has taken since the relatively inoffensive days of Raj Kapoor.

After her return home from France, Sumitra edited several more of Lester's films. She won a number of national "Best Editor" awards, but ultimately decided she wanted to direct rather than edit. She notes that "with editing, you can only work with what you are given," and she therefore felt that directing would be a more creative process. However, her first directing venture took a while to come to fruition. As Sumitra comments, "a writer can write (and find the publisher later), a painter can paint, but a filmmaker needs financial and other backing to start and complete a film." Eventually, Lester sold a thirty-acre coconut plantation to finance her first film, *Gehenu Lamai* (Girls), which was released in 1978. Sumitra remarks amusedly that they would have been quite rich now, if they had not sold that property! It turned out to be money well spent, however, as *Gehenu Lamai* was widely acclaimed, and won several national and international awards.

The film marked a brilliant entry into directing for Sumitra, and into acting for its lead actress, Vasanthi Chaturani. In fact, Sumitra's discovery of Vasanthi Chaturani reveals much about her instinctual talent for filmmaking. For her first film, Sumitra wanted an unknown lead actress, who was "unspoilt" and not associated with commercial success. She saw the young Vasanthi in a corridor when she visited a convent school in Gampaha. Though Vasanthi had never acted before, Sumitra simply had a hunch that she could act. With the permission of the Sister in charge of the convent, Sumitra engaged Vasanthi in the cast of *Gehenu Lamai*, guiding her throughout

Sumitra and Lester James Peries after returning from France, Colombo, 2001

Movie poster for her first film Gehenu Lamai, 1978

the production and helping her to develop as an actress. Sumitra laments that although there is now less of a cultural bias against becoming an actress or entering into the film and television industries, some schools still forbid their students from even appearing on screen.

Sumitra emulated her directorial success in *Gehenu Lamai* in several later films, including in *Ganga Addara* (By the River), *Yahalu Yeheli* (Friends), *Loku Duwa* (Eldest Daughter) and *Duwata Mawaka Misa* (A Mother Alone). Her films have been commended at major international film festivals, such as the London Film Festival, and critically acclaimed for their rare blend of artistry and realism. While she acknowledges that awards reaffirm artistic ability and that such recognition provides another dimension to one's work, Sumitra has consistently chosen her films on creative instinct rather than for the sake of garnering awards. Similarly, she has not regarded filmmaking as a means of making a lot of money and comments that she has "lived more from savings of the family than from what she has earned." For Sumitra, filmmaking is a means to "reconnect with your soul." As she explains, "You live amongst people in various communities, from different social strata … And in a way, it brings back the culture that you may have otherwise grown away from."

Sumitra Peries' films have centred on Sri Lankan village life. Though she would not necessarily like to live in a village (because, for instance, she would miss contact with urban intellectuals), she feels enriched by what she has learned of the intricacies of village life; for example, of elaborate coming-of-age rituals and 'slash and burn' methods of cultivation. She recounts admiringly how villagers recite incantations to rid the land of insects and serpents, while at the same time apologising to these creatures for having to do this and telling them, "it is only because the family needs to eat". As Sumitra observes, this is a very authentic form of environmental awareness!

It is not only through filmmaking that Sumitra has contributed to Sri Lankan cultural life. In the 1980s, she was a member of the Presidential Commission which conducted an inquiry into Sri Lanka's film industry. Sumitra also later served on the Board of Management of the Institute of Aesthetic Studies, at Kelaniya University. In 1995, her life took on a new dimension when she was appointed as Sri Lanka's permanent delegate to UNESCO, a post she held for four years while concurrently serving as Sri Lanka's ambassador to France and Spain. Sumitra remarks that it was a challenge to take on this new professional role when she was almost at retiring age! But her pioneering spirit and work in the film industry, as well as a lifetime of being exposed to different environments and challenges, helped Sumitra succeed in her diplomatic work. She had, for example, prior experience in marketing her films abroad, and in giving talks and interviews about her work and the film industry in Sri Lanka. Coming from a political family also helped her understand and navigate the international political arena. Since her youth, she has always been acutely aware that individuals and countries do not live in isolation but rather, are inevitably affected by world events.

When asked whether she has any regrets in life, Sumitra is hard-pressed to think of any. She has sometimes wondered if she should have had children; in the beginning she and Lester postponed starting a family and then it never ended up happening. But she also recognises that if they had had children, she may not have been able to pursue her filmmaking with such passion, since her focus would have been different. Besides, she feels fortunate to have a number of affectionate nieces and nephews.

Sumitra is encouraging of young women who are considering entering the film industry as she believes it is a career path which can give them confidence and encourage their self-expression. As Sumitra elucidates, "With each film, you bring a new experience and see life – and even yourself – through a new set of characters." Reflecting on her own experience, she believes that filmmaking has enabled her to connect with people in a much more meaningful way than if she had pursued a different career for purely financial reasons. However, while the opportunities for acting and directing in Sri Lanka are greater now than when she became a filmmaker, she cautions that it is still difficult to obtain a solid training in the field. While one would hope that there will be more schools in Sri Lanka that will provide such training, it is still necessary to rely largely on one's own initiative and resources. She therefore would advise young people to acquire some training abroad if they can.

Sumitra's work and artistic philosophy stand in welcome contrast to the commercialism and self-aggrandisement which have long pervaded the film industry, both in Sri Lanka and abroad. Rather, her life and work represent an inspirational model of independent thinking and artistic integrity, which have refused to be swayed by pecuniary incentives or conventional values.

Vajira Dias in Ravana - Pooja Dance, 1949

Vajira Dias
Kandyan Dancer

The name Vajira has come to be synonymous with Sri Lankan classical dancing. Born on 15 March 1932, as Vajira Perera, she is widely considered to be Sri Lanka's most gifted female dancer, and certainly one of the country's most treasured icons. Her grace and presence on stage have captivated audiences in Sri Lanka and around the world. With her extraordinary ability, Vajira paved the way for other women to enter the field of Kandyan dancing, which was traditionally regarded as a male domain. She succeeded in introducing a new feminine form of dance to the stage, hitherto unseen in Sri Lanka, thus unfolding a new era of creative opportunity for talented girls and women in the country.

In common with many celebrated achievers, Vajira was influenced by several people close to her. As a child, it was her mother Lilian – a very artistic person herself – who exerted a major influence on Vajira. Vajira's maternal grandfather had died at an early age, and his untimely death prevented her mother from pursuing her own talents. Vajira recalls that in that era, women were regarded as the *shakthi* (strength) in the home and it was generally the mother, as matriarch, who told them what to do. In any case, her father was a quiet personality and did not interfere in their upbringing. It was therefore not surprising that the young Vajira was raised and directed in accordance with her mother's wishes.

As a schoolteacher at Kalutara Vidyalaya, Vajira's mother was involved in producing plays and other dramas. She successfully convinced the school principal to introduce dancing as a subject and then compelled Vajira to follow the dancing classes, much against her daughter's will. Vajira's early training at Kalutara Vidyalaya, and later at Kalutara Balika Vidyalaya, was under the tutelage of Anandalal Athukorale, and Nimal Welgama. At the time, Vajira did not enjoy dancing, but the constant pressure from her mother ensured she showed up at classes and participated in school performances. One such performance was at the Kalutara Town Hall in 1943, in which she danced solo for the first time in a variety entertainment show.

It was soon apparent that Vajira was a talented young dancer who moved with natural ease and ability. Whenever she performed in school plays, the audience never failed to comment on her capabilities. Many of them told her mother that Vajira ought to be learning from

Chitrasena, the guru of dance from Colombo. As Vajira's mother naturally wished the best for her daughter, she arranged for Chitrasena (whom Vajira refers to as "Chitra") to come to Kalutara and teach a group of students at their home.

When dance lessons began at the Pereras' home in Kalutara, Vajira's sister, relatives, and friends all participated enthusiastically. But Vajira was a mischievous girl who had no interest in spending her time at these classes with Chitrasena. "I was naughty and wanted to play," says Vajira. "So when he came to teach, I used to run and hide!" She recalls how she did not like Chitrasena and used to call him "Mahasona", which meant *yaka* (devil) – even though, with a twinkling in her eye, she admits that he looked handsome in his black Indian *sherwarni*. Throughout this period, with her mother steadfastly pushing and urging her, she continued to attend his classes.

Chitrasena (born Maurice Dias) hailed from a thespian family. His father was an actor and producer who embraced the literature of Shakespeare and played Shakespearean characters, apparently loving the role of Shylock in the Merchant of Venice. Their home resembled a cultural centre of sorts, and Chitrasena's father encouraged his son to dance and act from a young age. In such an environment, Chitrasena was naturally drawn to the performing arts and in particular, to Indian dance and culture. He was an avid follower of his contemporary, Uday Shankar, the celebrated Indian dancer and choreographer who was known as a great showman at the time. Chitrasena's spirited nature was evident even as a youngster, when he introduced the Indian-style *kurta* dress to Sri Lanka and sported long hair, which did not go down too well with his family and relatives!

Chitrasena promoted and developed the Kandyan dance from the more traditional *Kohomba Kankari*, which is a ritualistic dance and a form of worship. He was most inspired and enthralled by Uday Shankar's feature of a 'dance with a story'. Chitrasena embraced and cultivated this very feature to elevate the position of Kandyan dance in Sri Lanka. He became the first professional dancer in Sri Lanka, launching his career in 1943. Yet his career was not without obstacles. One of the most difficult tasks was to demonstrate to Sri Lankan society that dance was a respectable profession, just as it was in India and many other countries. His efforts were gradually rewarded and the elite of society in Colombo began to pay attention to his talents. Dance soon became fashionable within wealthy and creative circles, and the public in general came to honour it as a profession.

With his artistic insights, Chitrasena quickly spotted star potential in the teenage

Vajira and Chitrasena, 1948

First female Kandyan dance costume designed by Somabandu

Vajira and set about convincing her family to come to Colombo. It was Vajira's older sister who came first to Colombo, to study medicine. Vajira joined her sister in 1946 and the two were accommodated in Chitrasena's house in Colpetty. Vajira attended Methodist College, completing her secondary school education at seventeen when she passed the Junior Cambridge examination. Immediately upon arriving in Colombo, Vajira also joined Chitrasena's school of dance – the Chitrasena *Kalayathanaya* – that had been established in 1944. It was here that she gradually began to enjoy dancing. She attended all the evening classes, after the end of her own school day. Her brilliance and ability surfaced quickly, and it did not take long for her to be singled out as the exemplary student in class who was called to the front row to lead the others.

The year 1948 was a memorable year for Vajira. She performed as the deer in Chitrasena's *Ramayanaya* during the Pageant of Lanka, an event organised to commemorate the historic occasion of Sri Lanka's national independence that year. This was an exciting moment for Vajira, as it was her first major public appearance on stage. Another of her early performances followed the next year, when she appeared in the opening Pooja dance in the ballet *Ravana*. Dressed in a beautiful white costume that comprised a three tiered frilled skirt, Vajira graced the stage with pride, wearing the first female costume for the Kandyan dance designed by Somabandu.

Though it was her mother who had introduced her to dancing, Vajira became increasingly influenced and guided by the leading light of Chitrasena. Chitrasena succeeded in instilling in Vajira a motivation and drive to dance, changing her mindset to the extent that dancing became inextricably linked to her everyday life. Being her senior, Chitrasena promoted Vajira's long-term interests and development. This was the era when Russians dominated the world of dance with great artists like Anna Pavlova and Vaslav Nijinsky. Chitrasena was constantly familiarising Vajira with such acclaimed dancers, giving her books on them to read and absorb. The renowned American dancer Martha Graham was also a contemporary, and her influence on Chitrasena grew after Graham herself visited Sri Lanka in 1956.

Before long, the reputation and stature of the unique combination of 'Chitrasena and Vajira' became known around the country. Together they introduced a creative and contemporary flavour to traditional dance forms. With this mutual development of their artistic goals and interests, their own personal relationship also blossomed, and it did not take long for Chitrasena and Vajira to fall in love. In 1950, Chitrasena married his star pupil when she was eighteen years old, thus sealing one of the greatest and best-loved artistic unions in the history of Sri Lanka. Quite characteristically, the young couple chose to attire themselves in traditional Kandyan dance costumes, complete with ornate jewellery, for their memorable wedding ceremony.

When asked about her most important achievement and greatest contribution to Sri Lankan dance, Vajira unhesitatingly responds, "It was the introduction of the female style of dancing." In what was generally regarded as a male domain, she underwent the same training in turns and jumps that men performed. She trained for years, and once she mastered the fundamental techniques, she realised there were elements of femininity that came naturally to a woman from an emotional perspective. Even so, initially she found it difficult to express emotion on stage, given that females were regarded as inherently shy and self-conscious. Besides, she found it was a natural instinct to represent your own self. One day, Chitrasena told her, "Forget the Vajira inside and just bring out the character." And yet as Vajira notes, "To bring about that transformation was not so simple."

Chitrasena was a very strict dance instructor and Vajira remembers days when she felt humiliated and would burst into tears. She was nevertheless well aware that Chitrasena strived to bring out the best in his students. His persistent guidance and tough discipline triggered a steely resolve in Vajira to somehow overcome whatever obstacles she faced in her training. She finally succeeded, expressing herself with a delicate beauty and style that contributed a totally new dimension to Sri Lankan dance.

Vajira's accomplishments and on-stage appeal continued to blossom and upon leaving school she became the first female professional dancer in Sri Lanka. Vajira recalls that even though females were introduced to the stage around 1948, other women had not chosen it as a career. The timing was right for the acceptance of female performing artists, for by that time, society had already undergone many changes; and largely as a result of Chitrasena's efforts, the public had begun to accept dance as a career even for women. Dance was introduced as a subject in many schools' curricula and it became fashionable to learn the national dance.

Motivated by her ambition to improve the Kandyan dance, Vajira trained arduously. She progressed to play the heroine in ballets produced by Chitrasena's school, and enjoyed her dancing every step of the way. The year 1952 was a momentous one for Vajira. She was the lead dancer as Prakirthi in the ballet *Chandalika*. It was also the year in which she produced her first children's ballet, *Kumudini*, performed in the first open-air theatre that was completed in the premises of the Chitrasena *Kalayathanaya* in 1951.

Karadiya was undeniably the most successful ballet which Chitrasena and Vajira brought to the stage. Vajira recalls that Chitrasena created *Karadiya* in 1961 especially for her, to play the main character 'Sisi' and to express the feminine aspect of the story. Naturally, Chitrasena also played a leading role, displaying his superb abilities in dance. *Karadiya* was the first successful example in Sri Lanka of a 'story in movement' brought to stage with a *corps de ballet* (non-principal dancers who help to portray the story). The overwhelmingly positive reception of this ballet had much to do with its style of presentation, as well as the high calibre of dancers.

Karadiya was also the first ballet to encompass theatre and stagecraft, and it was with this production that lighting and sets were introduced to students at the dance school. This new development presented Vajira with the opportunity to learn the art of choreography – an area which she learned and mastered, becoming a choreographer at the tender age of twenty. Her choreographic role further demonstrated that, although Vajira and Chitrasena worked in unison, Vajira was an independent creator. Few women dancers around the world had the distinction of combining dance and choreography. The productions of *Gini Hora*, staged in 1968, and *Berahanda*, staged in 2001 and directed by Vajira, were perhaps her most successful choreographed works.

In addition to her stature as a performer and a choreographer, Vajira has been recognised as an excellent dance teacher in her own right. Teaching at the *Kalayathanaya* and several leading schools, she has imparted her practical knowledge and creative brilliance to hundreds of students over the course of several decades. Her tremendous contributions to Sri Lankan dance have been acknowledged with many awards, including the Presidential Award Kala Suri in 1988, as well the International Women's Day Contribution to the Dance of Sri Lanka awards in 1988 and 1998.

Vajira has performed abroad several times during her distinguished career. Her first overseas tour was to the USSR in 1957, where she was the lead dancer in the ballet *Sama Vijaya* (Triumph of Peace, depicting the destruction caused by the atom bomb) at a youth festival sponsored by the World Peace Council. This was only the beginning of her overseas travels, and since then, her performances have been seen and enjoyed around the globe, including in several countries in Europe, as well as in Australia, Canada, India and many other Asian countries.

Thus the Kandyan dance, the heritage of

all Sri Lankans, became known to the world, gracefully expressed through Vajira's slender figure and beautiful eyes. During those years, she captivated diverse audiences – which included members of royalty, Presidents, Prime Ministers and many other foreign dignitaries – with her mastery of the art. As might be expected, not all of their tours proceeded perfectly smoothly. Vajira recollects how she twisted her ankle during their second tour to the USSR in 1963. Having performed in agony on the opening night, it was left to her sister Vipuli, a very talented dancer herself who also made dancing a career, to continue in Vajira's role the next night. When asked what she believes was their most successful overseas performance, she responds: "It was at St Gallen in Switzerland when *Karadiya* was staged. The audience never stopped clapping and we had so many curtain calls!" She says this in a simple and unaffected manner, an endearing characteristic of this great lady.

In 1951, motherhood dawned with the birth of a baby girl, Upeka. A second child, Anjalika, was born two years later, and in the same year, her second children's ballet, *Himakumariya* was created. Their son Anudatta was born in 1957, and as one would expect in that era, it was an occasion for rejoicing in the family. So how did Vajira manage to balance her personal life and career with such composure and dedication? Throughout

The role of mother in Chandalika, 50th anniversary celebration

all of this, she continued dancing and teaching, even performing on stage into the sixth month of her pregnancies. As was customary in Sri Lanka, she received tremendous support from her mother and also her sister. Above all, she managed to skillfully integrate dance into the normal family routine.

Her mother loved to watch Vajira dance and would seize any opportunity to come and see Vajira perform. It so happened that they were never too far from each other, and even lived in adjoining houses in her latter years, thus allowing her mother ready access to Vajira. Having played the pivotal role in pushing Vajira into the dancing world and giving her support and encouragement throughout her career, she died at the age of 99; fittingly, with Vajira by her side.

The year 1996 was the highlight of Vajira's life so far and certainly a reason to celebrate and reflect. It was the 50th anniversary of Vajira's dancing career. The ballet *Chandalika*, choreographed and presented by Vajira, was staged to commemorate the event, with Vajira in the role of mother and Upeka in the role of daughter.

Vajira's advice to other aspiring dancers is that, most importantly, one must be a good dancer and dedicated to it. One should also adjust family life to suit one's career. Indeed, there is no necessity to remain unmarried, for example, since dance ought to be embodied in family life. Her wise and practical approach is perhaps the underlying reason that her children Upeka and Anjalika are also recognised and well known dancers. Today, Upeka is one of the foremost dancers in Sri Lanka and the leading soloist of the Chitrasena ensemble. Anjalika is known not only as a vibrant and creative performer but also a teacher and choreographer of rare excellence. Vajira's son Anudatta adds his contribution as a sound engineer, reproducing music electronically with great skill. Her daughter-in-law Janaki is an extremely talented artist, as are her granddaughters, Heshma, Udamanthi and Thajithangani, who are blossoming and showing promising signs of being able to continue the legacy of their grandparents.

Commenting on the facilities for dancing in the country, Vajira mentions that the University of Fine Arts provides training and there are many young girls and boys that follow their program (in addition to the *Kalayathanaya*). Yet she finds that students use such university education and training as a means to obtain a teaching certificate, rather than to dance on stage and launch a professional career.

It is a pity that, since 1998, a foot injury has prevented Vajira from continuing to perform on stage. This, however, has not in any way dampened her spirits or hampered her other work. She continues to breathe dance and music, and lives with other dancers like an extended family, feeling fortunate to play the role of matriarch to the younger generation and blessed that she is never alone. Constantly surrounded by a large group of people who love dance, she plays an important role in continuing to promote the art for both men and women. She founded the *Preserve the Dance Project* in 2000 to assist the men, having noticed the dwindling number of male dancers in the country. She also promotes the health and well-being of many by conducting dance exercise classes in her home. Vajira's regular contact with younger generations is likely a key ingredient that helps her to maintain her effervescent personality and youthful appearance well into her seventies.

Vajira's long career in dancing has been uniquely infused with love and dedication. Her philosophy of dancing to improve and develop the style of dance, without dwelling on monetary aspects, has made the journey that she began as a teenager an exhilarating and rewarding experience. There is no doubt that her remarkable achievements and contributions are now indelibly carved into Sri Lanka's cultural history.

Notes

Bhikkuni Kusuma

The reference to the road "less traveled by" is from: Robert Frost, 'The Road Not Taken', 1916.

On the restoration of Bhikkuni Order (sic) – Selected articles, at www.viet.net/~anson/ebud/ebdha220.htm.

Kumari Jayawardena

Amrita Chhachhi, "Reflections: Kumari Jayawardena", *Development and Change* 37 (6), 1335–1346 (2006).

Radhika Coomaraswamy, "A tribute to Kumari Jayawardena – 'Mother of all mothers'", *Daily Mirror*, 29 November 2007.

Feminist Theory Website: Kumari Jayawardena, at www.cddc.vt.edu/feminism/Jayawardena.html.

Maureen Seneviratne

Randima Attygalle, "Delivering justice the graceful way", *The Nation*, 1 July 2007, at www.nation.lk/2007/07/01/eyefea3.htm.

Dr Stella de Silva

Department of Paediatrics, Faculty of Medicine, University of Colombo, Sri Lanka, History, at www.cmb.ac.lk/academic/medicine/ext_pages/Paediatrics/history.html.

Stella G de Silva, "Development of paediatrics in Sri Lanka", Sri Lanka Journal of Child Health, 30(4), 85-86 (2001).

The Sri Lanka College of Paediatricians, History and the Current status of the College, at www.slcp.slt.lk/pgs/history.htm.

Sri Lanka Medical Association, *A Brief History of the SLMA*, at www.slma.lk/history.html.

Manouri P. Senanayake, *Paediatrics and Child Care in Sri Lanka: The Past Unfolded*, Vijitha Yapa Publications, 2007.

Hilary Abeyaratne, *A Life in the Round – Desamanya Kamalika: The girl from Giruwa Pattuwa*, WHT Publications, Colombo, 2006.

Nanda P. Wanasundera, *The Island (Leisure)*, 8 June 2008, at www.island.lk/2008/06/08/leisure1.html.